THE REMEDY

Exercising God's Authority in Your Life

D0104432

BILL & MICHAEL FRENCH

FOREWORD BY JOHN PAUL JACKSON

Endorsements

The Remedy weaves together biblical truths with the pragmatic to get Kingdom results. From the very beginning it takes us on a journey on how to set those captives free. *The Remedy* brings language and understanding to Jesus' statement, "He who the Son sets free is free indeed." A must-read for every believer.

—AARON EVANS
Vice President of Ministry Outreach and Operations,
Streams Ministries International

I consider this book to be a significant tool to prepare the people of God to advance in victory. It is enlightening as well as equipping. With a rich history in spiritual deliverance, Bill and Michael French have put together an awesome tool to help anyone who is serious about advancing the Kingdom of God. This book is a refreshing combination of revelatory insights and Scripture-based information, equipping the Body of Christ to stand firm in the victory provided by Christ Jesus. This is a timely and significant book. I wholeheartedly recommend not only the reading but also the implementation of these guidelines for victory.

—BOBBY CONNER
Founder, Eagle's View Ministries

With the edge of experience, *The Remedy* is not merely another good book on spiritual warfare. It contains tested wisdom needed to overcome your strong enemy. Beware: The contents inside are lethal and dangerous to the powers of darkness.

—JIM GOLL
Cofounder, Encounters Network
Author of *The Seer, Praying for Israel's Destiny*,
and *Elijah's Revolution*

It was with much anticipation that I looked forward to reading *The Remedy*. Bill and Michael French bring much hands-on experience as well as biblical insight with understanding into the realm of the Spirit. There is a present call extended to the Church to "come up here" to glean revelation and maturity essential for the end-time army of God. This book provides both. I highly recommend it for those who desire the high calling of God and fruitfulness in His Kingdom.

—PAUL KEITH DAVIS
Founder, WhiteDove Ministries

This book is a balanced, biblical, and long-overdue treatment of a subject that has a history of abuse. The authors have carefully redressed the issue of spiritual warfare in a manner that will bless all who read it. *The Remedy* and John Paul Jackson's *Needless Casualties of War* go hand in hand and will encourage those who have been confused in the area of deliverance. It is an excellent introduction to the subject and will particularly bless those who have struggled with fear of the devil rather than confidence in God.

—R. T. KENDALL
Former Senior Minister,
Westminster Chapel, London, England

†HE
REmEDY

Exercising God's Authority in Your Life

BILL AND MICHAEL FRENCH

Streams Publishing House
North Sutton, New Hampshire

Requests for permissions should be addressed to:
Streams Publishing House
P.O. Box 550
North Sutton, New Hampshire 03260
Tel: 603.927.4224
www.streamsministries.com

To contact the authors, please write:
Advocate Ministries
4445 Crescent Road
Birmingham, Alabama 35210

Unless otherwise noted, Scripture quotations are taken from the New King James Version, Copyright 1979, 1980, 1982 by Thomas Nelson, Inc., Publishers. Used by permission.

Creative Director and Managing Editor: Carolyn Blunk
Contributing Editor: Dorian Kreindler
Associate Editor: Lauren Stinton
Assistant Editor: Mary Ballotte
Editorial Assistant: Leslie Herrier
Cover designed by Ray Moore
Interior designed by Pat Reinheimer

ISBN 1-58483-1014

Library of Congress
2005933708

Printed in the United States of America.

FOR MORE INFORMATION
ON STREAMS BOOKS AND OTHER MATERIALS,
CALL 1.888.441.8080 (USA AND CANADA)
OR 603.927.4224

We dedicate this book to our wives, Joyce and Elisa,
for their patience and commitment to us,
without which we would never have been able to
learn the principles contained in these pages.

Contents

Foreword

"Behold, I give you the authority to trample
on serpents and scorpions, and over all the
power of the enemy, and nothing shall by any
means hurt you."

—Luke 10:19

A believer's view of the demonic realm often falls into one
of three categories: One type sees a demon in every
shadow and ardently rebukes every cold draft. On the other
end of the spectrum, another type has adopted a "Christian-
cavalier" mind-set and doesn't believe we can be attacked or
even influenced by demons at all. Members of the third group
are afraid to even mention Satan's name, just in case he's listening and comes after them with a pitchfork. Fortunately,
none of these perspectives is accurate.

We are in a spiritual war. We fight this war every single day.
Each one of us is involved in a moment-by-moment battle
against an enemy that, for the most part, we don't see. We may
feel him. We may even smell him. But we don't usually see
him. His tactics are secretive, for that's how he works successfully: Once he has been exposed, he can be dealt with.

And that is the truth Satan desperately tries to hide: God has
given us authority over his power. Jesus didn't say, "I give you
authority to *tiptoe* over all the power of the enemy" (which
would have been sufficient), or, "I give you authority to *walk*
over all the power of the enemy." No, instead, Jesus declared, "I
give you authority to *trample* all the power of the enemy."

We serve a God who has more authority and power over the demonic realm than we could ever humanly imagine. Comparing His power to any other would be like comparing a B-2 Stealth Bomber to a child's paper airplane. Demons tremble at the mere mention of His name. However, for millennia, Satan has skillfully managed to overexert, blind, and scare many believers. We have experienced more than a little confusion over our God-given authority. Jesus never intended His bride to be wrapped up in, ignorant of, or scared of the demonic realm. Instead, He gave us authority to stand up to the devil's schemes and reveal his lies for what they truly are.

God's power and authority over the demonic realm are wonderfully displayed and fantastically obvious in the Gospels: One of Jesus' most prolific ministries on earth was that of deliverance, setting the captives free. The demon-possessed would see Him from far off, throw themselves at His feet, and try to distract or delay their departure by physically manifesting in their hosts. But He was not distractible; the enemy was still cast out.

Imagine walking with God to the extent that when the enemy sees the power of God in you, he panics and falls on his face. This is the authority Jesus wielded—the authority He granted us so we could trample the enemy's power. *The Remedy: Exercising God's Authority in Your Life* by my good friends Bill and Michael French will help everyone who reads it come to a better understanding of the sovereign power of our God, His absolute authority, and the spiritual weapons He has given us to turn back the battle at the gate.

—JOHN PAUL JACKSON
Founder, Streams Ministries International

Acknowledgments

We wish to acknowledge the hundreds of people who have trusted this ministry with their spiritual (and sometimes physical) lives as they endeavored to overcome the demonic realm.

It is also important to recognize the commitment of the staff of Advocate Ministries: Richard Martin, Leslee Hughes, and Paula Harris. We also want to acknowledge the staff of Cahaba Christian Fellowship: Jim Henderson, Shawn Lombard, Chase Thompson, Sam Knowles, and Yohanna Maginga. The staff from both these ministries have carried our burdens as the pages of this book were written.

We also recognize the Freedom Night Ministry Team. The individuals who have worked side by side with Bill over the years are too numerous to count. These men and women stand with us and beside us in all we do, never flinching in the face of spiritual warfare. Learning and implementing the principles described here have subjected us and those around us to many attacks of the enemy, but he has never been victorious.

We would also like to thank John Paul Jackson, Greg and Patty Mapes, and the entire team at Streams Ministries. Without your help, this project might never have gone beyond Michael's computer screen.

Finally, these acknowledgments would not be complete without recognizing the commitment and contribution to this project by Carolyn Blunk. Her insight and creativity helped this book come to life. The recent loss of Carolyn will have lasting impact on our lives.

Knowing Our Enemy:

Biblical Foundations

Deliverance ministry is a touchy subject for most of the Church world. Just mention the word *deliverance*, and many people conjure up images of *The Exorcist* and other media stereotypes. The confusion, fear, and anxiety caused by these associations are a tactic of the enemy to keep people from understanding the depths of God's power. Deliverance doesn't need to be a scary subject—it just needs to be better understood. We need to replace the mythology surrounding deliverance with the reality of God's Word.

Section One of this book deals with the foundational biblical elements of deliverance ministry. It will answer questions such as:

- Are the devil and demons real?
- If so, what do they do?
- What impact does this have on me as a Christian?

In order to understand deliverance ministry and its place in the contemporary Church, we need to begin with a biblical definition and show why deliverance is a valid and necessary ministry.

CHAPTER 1

Who Is
Our Enemy?

Over the years, many people have argued that it is inappropriate to discuss the topic of knowing our enemy. They feel that time spent discussing the devil glorifies him instead of God, but it is important to remember that only the untrained soldier does not seek to understand his or her adversary.

God's Word repeatedly compares the believer to a soldier actively engaged in warfare (Philippians 2:25; 2 Timothy 2:3–4). It is important to know that one aspect of being a competent soldier in God's army requires recognizing the nature of the enemy and his tactics, as well as what motivates him to steal, kill, and destroy.

THE ORIGIN OF SATAN

God's Word provides a limited amount of information regarding Satan's origin. Isaiah 14 and Ezekiel 28 present the idea that Satan, once known as Lucifer, existed before the events of Genesis. At the time, Jewish authors used a device called parallel semantics, which enabled two histories to be narrated as one. For example, Isaiah 14 tells the story of the Babylonian kingdom, an ancient kingdom that was evil and corrupt. But these verses also describe the fall of Lucifer and how he became Satan. In Ezekiel 28, we find the story of the kingdom of Tyre, an equally evil and corrupt nation. Here, too, is the story of Lucifer's fall. Both chapters describe two subjects (Lucifer and the kingdoms) in one writing.

Based on these two chapters, it appears that Lucifer was a powerful angel (on a similar level as Michael) who sought to exalt himself to the level of God; instead, he fell from Heaven.

If Gabriel is identified as the great messenger angel and Michael as the great warrior angel, then Lucifer would be identified as the great worship angel.

> The workmanship of your timbrels and pipes
> Was prepared for you on the day you were created.
> —EZEKIEL 28:13

This verse associates Lucifer with music and worship. When we examine Satan's activities on the earth today, we recognize that one of his primary tools is music and its influence on humankind.

The beginning verses of Ezekiel 28 indicate that Lucifer was a beautiful being:

> Every precious stone was your covering:
> The sardius, topaz, and diamond,
> Beryl, onyx, and jasper,
> Sapphire, turquoise, and emerald with gold.
> —EZEKIEL 28:13

> "Your heart was lifted up because of your beauty;
> You corrupted your wisdom for the sake of your splendor."
> —EZEKIEL 28:17

Satan's beauty was one of the causes of his downfall. Whether or not one accepts that Lucifer was beautiful and musical, these verses from Ezekiel 28 and Isaiah 14 clearly indicate several other details.

First, Lucifer was a powerful being. Isaiah 14:12 not only identifies Lucifer's fall but goes on to describe he who is "cut down to the ground" as he "who weakened the nations." Lucifer was one

> "'. . . who made the earth tremble,
> Who shook kingdoms,
> Who made the world as a wilderness
> And destroyed its cities.'"
>
> —ISAIAH 14:16–17

Second, Lucifer had authority:

> "For you have said in your heart:
> 'I will ascend into heaven,
> I will exalt my throne above the stars of God;
> I will also sit on the mount of the congregation
> On the farthest sides of the north;
> I will ascend above the heights of the clouds,
> I will be like the Most High.'"
>
> —ISAIAH 14:13–14

Lucifer boasts that he will exalt his throne above the stars of God. What does a throne symbolize? Authority and dominion. It is this attitude of pride (notice the phrase *I will* appears five times in these two verses) that results in Lucifer's downfall. He believed that he could be "like the Most High," that he could be equal with God.

Third, Satan was persuasive. He convinced one-third of the host of Heaven that he could be equal with God. He lured them to follow him in rebellion and, ultimately, to be cast out with him (Revelation 12:4–9).

SATAN'S PRIMARY ROLE IN THE EARTH

Isaiah 14 and Ezekiel 28 describe who Satan was before the fall. However, this book focuses more on what he is doing in the present. Romans 11:29 teaches us that "the gifts and the calling of God are irrevocable." According to this scriptural principle, Satan may very well retain much of the power, authority, and persuasiveness he was given as Lucifer, a highly attractive being.

God's Word also refers to "all the power of the enemy" (Luke 10:19) and Satan transforming himself "into an angel of light" (2 Corinthians 11:14). If Satan maintains at least some of the power, authority, and persuasiveness he operated in prior to the fall, believers must be prepared for the deployment of those skills today.

Zechariah 3 offers the first clue to how Satan's purposes operate in the earth. Let's look at the cleansing of Joshua, the high priest:

> Then he showed me Joshua the high priest standing before the Angel of the LORD, and Satan standing at his right hand to oppose him.
>
> —ZECHARIAH 3:1

It is unlikely that any of us individually is important enough for Satan to come in person to oppose us. Yet, opposition to God's servants is a huge priority of Satan and his minions.

Satan is not omnipotent, omniscient, and omnipresent as are God the Father, Son, and Holy Spirit. However, since one-third of the heavenly host fell with him, he does have sufficient help all over the globe and in the Heavens to oppose God's servants.

When we as believers decide to walk more closely with the Lord in loving obedience, to faithfully act in conjunction with God's call on our lives, we can reasonably assume Satan (or more likely, one of his representatives) will oppose us. So, it becomes extremely important for us not only to know our enemy, but to know ourselves and the authority in which God has designed us to walk. The believer's authority will be discussed more fully in Chapter Five.

SATAN'S PRIMARY TOOL

Satan, the adversary, makes his first appearance to Adam and Eve in Genesis 3. He comes in the form of a serpent with language ability. He is probably standing upright, since he will shortly be cast down to crawl upon the earth. Adam and Eve are still walking in innocence and clothed in nothing more than the glory of the Lord. However, something is about to happen that will forever strip them of their innocence and reveal their nakedness.

This is the story of the first Adam's loss of his kingdom to the devious and persuasive serpent, Satan. We see that Satan's powers of persuasion are cloaked in innuendo, half-truths, and lies. He consistently uses these tactics to oppose God's servants. He weaves these lies well and seeks to subtly cast doubt upon God's Word.

Now the serpent was more cunning than any beast of the field which the LORD God had made. And he

said to the woman, "Has God indeed said, 'You shall
not eat of every tree of the garden'?" And the woman
said to the serpent, "We may eat the fruit of the trees
of the garden; but of the fruit of the tree which is in
the midst of the garden, God has said, 'You shall not
eat it, nor shall you touch it, lest you die.'" Then the
serpent said to the woman, "You will not surely die.
For God knows that in the day you eat of it your
eyes will be opened, and you will be like God,
knowing good and evil."

—GENESIS 3:1–5

In Satan's first deception, he asks, "Is it really true? Has
God *really* said you cannot eat from every tree in the garden?" This was not what God had said to Adam and Eve, but
now Satan has a base from which to work. He immediately
begins to question God's meaning: "Does God really care
about you? If He did, wouldn't He let you eat from all the
trees? Do you really believe you would die if you ate from
this tree?" This mind-set of selfish ambition casts doubt and
suspicion on God's Word. It is the primary tool the enemy
uses to oppose those who choose to serve Almighty God.
However, though Satan casts doubt and suspicion at every
turn, God's Word cannot fail.

Satan's final ploy was a direct attack on God's Word: "You
will not surely die." Yet spiritual death came immediately,
and physical death became the common experience of
humanity. While some still question the accuracy of the
account because Adam's physical death did not occur on that
literal day, the Bible states, "With the Lord one day is as a
thousand years" (2 Peter 3:8). From that time on, no person
ever lived beyond a thousand years. This verse also makes

one other thing abundantly clear: God exists outside our understanding of time. The passage continues:

> The Lord is not slack concerning His promise, as some count slackness, but is longsuffering toward us, not willing that any should perish but that all should come to repentance.
>
> —2 PETER 3:9

CAN SATAN READ YOUR MIND?

If Satan cannot oppose God's chosen ones through deception, then his next endeavor is to kill them. Genesis 3 explains why Satan seeks to destroy God's servants:

> "And I will put enmity
> Between you and the woman,
> And between your seed and her Seed;
> He shall bruise your head,
> And you shall bruise His heel."
>
> —GENESIS 3:15

Satan's efforts to destroy the woman's Seed reveal another important piece of information about our adversary. Genesis 3:15 contains the first prophecy of the coming Messiah: The Seed of the woman "shall bruise your head, and you shall bruise His heel." To Satan, Cain and Abel appeared to be the Seed of the woman, so he provoked Cain to kill Abel. Satan was trying to kill the Seed, but he failed.

When Moses was born and the spirit world began to sense the excitement of a deliverer arriving upon the scene, Satan assumed Moses was the Seed. Satan entered the heart of

Pharaoh and compelled him to seek to kill all the Hebrew male infants. Neither Satan's nor Pharaoh's plans succeeded.

Next, we see the true Messiah born in a manger in Bethlehem. Once again, Satan struck out against the children, and once again he was unsuccessful. Each time God prepared to bring forth a mighty work of deliverance, Satan sought to kill the children. He used this strategy in an attempt to destroy the Seed—the Deliverer, God's Servant—who would be the vessel to bring forth freedom.

Today, thousands of children are killed each year at the hands of abortionists. Does our adversary again feel that something is on the horizon in the spiritual world?

What we learn from this is clear: Satan cannot read your mind. If he could, he would not have failed in finding Jesus. Unquestionably, certain people knew who and where the Messiah was. Mary and Joseph knew. So did Elizabeth and the shepherds. Yet Satan failed as a result of imperfect knowledge. He could not read the minds of those who knew the Christ, and he cannot read the minds of men and women today. He has, however, had thousands of years to become an expert on human behavior. He will use this knowledge to attempt to persuade men and women that he knows exactly what they are thinking and give credibility to the subtle lies he uses so well.

ARE THERE LIMITS TO SATAN'S AUTHORITY?

Satan opposes God's servants primarily through deception; however, he is not all-powerful. There are limits to Satan's authority. We find an excellent reference in the book of Job that answers this question and also provides other insights about the areas from which Satan operates.

The first thing we learn is that Satan still has access to God's throne.

Now there was a day when the sons of God came to
present themselves before the LORD, and Satan also
came among them. And the LORD said to Satan,
"From where do you come?" So Satan answered the
LORD and said, "From going to and fro on the earth,
and from walking back and forth on it."

—JOB 1:6–7

Satan has been going to and fro on the earth and has now
come to present himself before the Lord. This Scripture provides significant information when we recognize that Satan
operates both on earth and in heavenly realms, but more
important is what comes next:

Then the LORD said to Satan, "Have you considered
My servant Job, that there is none like him on the
earth, a blameless and upright man, one who fears
God and shuns evil?" So Satan answered the LORD
and said, "Does Job fear God for nothing? Have You
not made a hedge around him, around his house-
hold, and around all that he has on every side? You
have blessed the work of his hands, and his posses-
sions have increased in the land. But now, stretch
out Your hand and touch all that he has, and he will
surely curse You to Your face!" And the LORD said
to Satan, "Behold, all that he has is in your power;
only do not lay a hand on his person." So Satan
went out from the presence of the LORD.

—JOB 1:8–12

Here we find clear proof that Satan's authority in connection with God's servants is limited.

Job 1 details an interesting exchange between God and Satan regarding Job. In that conversation, it is important to note that it was God, not Satan, who brought up the issue of Job. The Lord Himself points out His choice servant to the enemy. Satan reacts by asking permission to come against Job. This point is remarkable. Job is protected from the attacks of the enemy until Satan received permission to act, and even then his actions are limited—"only do not lay a hand on his person."

This isn't the only example of the Lord allowing the enemy to test His servant. Remember Peter's conversation with Jesus. The Lord said that Satan had asked permission to sift Peter as wheat (Luke 22:31). That request apparently had been granted, since the Lord reminded Peter that He had prayed for him, that his faith would not fail during the sifting process (Luke 22:32). Jesus further advised Peter that when he had returned to Him, he was to strengthen the believers. In effect, Jesus said, "Peter, I have allowed this! Satan can do what he wills, but he can go only so far. Afterward, Peter, you will return to Me." It was after this that Peter, who first denied Christ, became one of the pillars of the faith.

In the examples and circumstances of both Job and Peter, we find limitations on the authority Satan had in testing them. In both cases, Satan understood a line existed that he could not cross. Satan's authority to test and try was and still is limited. God had already set the limitations, and only He or Job could have extended them. If Job had complained in bitterness and rebellion, it would have extended the boundary of Satan's authority. Instead, Job endured and remained faithful. Having suffered what was sent against him, Job responded:

> "Naked I came from my mother's womb,
> And naked shall I return there.

The LORD gave, and the LORD has taken away;
Blessed be the name of the LORD."

—Job 1:21

Satan, knowing his limitations, later returned to the Lord and asked for the line to be moved (Job 2:3–6). Even after God increased the limits, Job didn't sin with his lips. He was confronted by his friends and his wife, and could have easily moved the line by saying, "This is too much," but instead he stood fast. Job embodied the commandment of Ephesians 6:13 in that he stood, and having done all, continued to stand.

Christians should not become confused or despondent when Satan is granted limited authority to *sift* them, for God will use the event to purify and prepare His vessels for greater use. Satan is the devourer who has come to steal, kill, and destroy. If we are walking in rebellion, we grant him access to wreak havoc. Even if we are living in obedience, there are times in our lives when God allows him to assault us, saying, "You have My permission, but you cannot go beyond this point." In times of testing, when we want to blame Satan, it is wise to first ask God if He is allowing this process to teach us. Job lost much, but in the end, the Lord restored to him twice as much as he'd had before. Why? First, Job stood and, having done all, continued to stand; and second, he turned away from selfishness.

And the LORD restored Job's losses when he prayed for his friends. Indeed the LORD gave Job twice as much as he had before.

—Job 42:10

Isaiah 14 and Ezekiel 28 paint a graphic picture of the being who would later be known as Satan. The biblical portrait of Satan is one many people would prefer not to see. Instead of a strong, authoritative, destructive being with tremendous powers of persuasion, the world chooses to see a somewhat foolish imp dressed in a red suit and carrying a pitchfork. This image is exactly what our enemy would like God's army to see. Through it, he has convinced many that he is a fairy tale, dead, or incompetent, and so he isn't perceived as a threat.

If we are to stand against the devil, we must expect him to oppose us at every turn and that his primary weapon will be deception (Zechariah 3). While Satan is not omnipresent and cannot read our mind, he still has access to the heavenly realms. He uses that access and his cunning to direct his forces against God's saints. So, why is he here at all? Wouldn't it be much easier on us if Satan didn't exist? Consider this—how would we grow if we had no adversary? A kitchen knife is not sharpened on a stick of butter, but rather against an abrasive stone. And so it is with our lives.

Demons and the Things They Do

B oth the Old and New Testaments attest to the existence of demons. Two Hebrew words are translated "demon" or "devil": (1) *shed*: a demon, malignant, devil (Deuteronomy 32:17; Psalm 106:37); and (2) *sair*: shaggy, a he-goat, faun, devil, or satyr (Leviticus 17:7; 2 Chronicles 11:15). The primary Greek word translated "demon" or "devil" in the New Testament is *daimonion*: a demonic being, a deity, devil, or god. From these and other scriptural references, it is clear that a demon is a spirit being that seeks to set itself up as a deity or god in individuals' lives. Its true intention is to bring about destruction (notice that the Hebrew word *shed* can also be translated "malignant").[1]

God's Word does not give the specific origin of demons. However, we can assume these beings are the third of the heavenly host that fell with Lucifer after he enticed them to follow him in his rebellion. We can also assume that Satan remains their leader. In fact, God's Word strongly suggests that demonic ranks are structured in military form with Satan as the head, chief, or general. Ephesians lays the foundation for this view:

> For we do not wrestle against flesh and blood, but
> against principalities, against powers, against the
> rulers of the darkness of this age, against spiritual
> hosts of wickedness in the heavenly places.
>
> —EPHESIANS 6:12

Though Scripture does not paint a precise picture of the demonic realm, we can glean much about demons and their actions from various passages. From this study of the demonic realm, one theme becomes clear: Demons follow the direction of their master, the devil, and seek to do his bidding. Satan came "to steal, and to kill, and to destroy" (John 10:10), and so these are the primary tasks of his minions also.

DO DEMONS STILL EXIST ON THE EARTH TODAY?

Some people still wonder whether demons exist in the world, but the pervasiveness and openness of occult activity is a sufficient answer to that question. For those who seek scriptural proof, God's Word contains much evidence of the continued existence and activity of demons.

Until the prophecies of John in the book of Revelation are fulfilled, Satan and his demonic hordes remain loosed upon the earth. Revelation 20 describes the ultimate fate of Satan and his forces, and most biblical scholars agree that the events leading to Satan's captivity have not yet been fulfilled. So, both present-day physical evidence and biblical prophecy confirm that demons remain loosed upon the earth and are presently active. It also seems that demons' activity may have taken on different manifestations but their goals and functions remain the same. The following scriptural examples support this view.

MEN FROM THE TOMBS

The reader can glean a great deal from Jesus' encounter with the two demon-possessed men in Matthew 8.

> When He had come to the other side, to the country of the Gergesenes, there met Him two demon-possessed men, coming out of the tombs, exceedingly fierce, so that no one could pass that way. And suddenly they cried out, saying, "What have we to do with You, Jesus, You Son of God? Have You come here to torment us before the time?" Now a good way off from them there was a herd of many swine feeding. So the demons begged Him, saying, "If you cast us out, permit us to go away into the herd of swine." And He said to them, "Go." So when they had come out, they went into the herd of swine. And suddenly the whole herd of swine ran violently down the steep place into the sea, and perished in the water. Then those who kept them fled; and they went away into the city and told everything, including what had happened to the demon-possessed men. And behold, the whole city came out to meet Jesus. And when they saw Him, they begged Him to depart from their region.
>
> —MATTHEW 8:28–34

This account provides insight about what demons do. Verse 28 begins by identifying these men as being "exceedingly fierce" or violent. These violent tendencies resulted from the demonic pressure overwhelming the men.

The passage then conveys that the men "cried out" or shouted (verse 29). This must have been demons speaking

through them, since the men themselves were not being tormented by Jesus. Significantly, the demons were able to detect
two points of information the people did not: (1) They recognized Jesus as the Son of God, and (2) there is an appointed
time for their torment.

Verse 31 confirms that demons were acting through these
men, since they petitioned Jesus about where they should be
sent. Apparently, demons have something akin to emotions or
feelings because they "begged" Jesus, pleading, "If You cast us out
. . ." There was never any question about Jesus' ability to drive
them out, so their statement was a delaying tactic. Certainly these
demons knew they had to go, but they didn't want to.

What might easily be overlooked in this account is where
the demons were found and then where they were sent.
When Jesus appeared on the scene, these demons were occu-
pying the bodies of men. We then learn that demons can
occupy or inhabit animal bodies as well ("they went into the
herd of swine"). These conclusions are still controversial, as
they were in Jesus' time; this deliverance wrought such
upheaval that "the whole city" came out and implored Jesus
to vacate their region.

Examination of this passage indicates one thing for certain: Demonic entities intend to destroy the lives of those
they seek to control. In this case, the two men were driven to
live apart from society in a very undesirable location (in the
midst of the tombs). While this lifestyle was certainly not
what these individuals would have chosen, they were manip-
ulated and coerced into it. This same destructive goal is being
pursued by demonic powers today.

An often-unwitting introduction to the demonic realm
occurs by using occult objects such as a Ouija board. While often
considered merely a game, this board accesses an immersion that

is far from innocent, no matter the context of its use. The following example shows how dabbling in "innocent" occult games can produce life-altering consequences.

Bill was asked by a psychiatrist who worked with his ministry to meet with a young woman seeking release from a psychiatric hospital. The woman explained that she did not desire to be in the psychiatric ward and added that her problems had originated from playing with a Ouija board. She quickly realized the board was actually answering her questions, and ultimately, the demonic entity controlling the board advised her that if she played a certain form of rock music, the board would become more effective. She did, and it did. Next, the board advised that if she would place some of her blood on it, it would become even more effective. Once again she did, and it did. In the end, her arms were covered with scars from this induced bloodletting, and she became a resident at an "undesirable" location, all through demonic manipulation.

SICKNESS AND DISEASE

The narrative in Matthew 9 provides additional information about what demons do.

> As they went out, behold, they brought to Him a
> man, mute and demon-possessed. And when the
> demon was cast out, the mute spoke. And the multi-
> tudes marveled, saying, "It was never seen like this
> in Israel!"
> —MATTHEW 9:32–33

In these verses, we learn that demons can render an individual mute. Notice Jesus did not say, "Be healed," but the verse records that "when the demon was cast out, the mute spoke."

Now, let's look at the account of the woman with the spirit of infirmity.

> And behold, there was a woman who had a spirit of
> infirmity eighteen years, and was bent over and
> could in no way raise herself up. But when Jesus saw
> her, He called her to Him and said to her, "Woman,
> you are loosed from your infirmity." And he laid His
> hands on her, and immediately she was made
> straight, and glorified God.
>
> —LUKE 13:11–13

Taken together, these verses show that demons have the power to cause sickness and disease. While we cannot infer that every illness is brought on by some demonic oppression, these passages demonstrate that inducing physical infirmities is one of the weapons demons use to destroy an individual. A number of other Scriptures confirm this demonic function, including Matthew 12:22 and Matthew 17:14–18.

Mark's gospel provides additional insight into the demonic world's ultimate goal. The following passage recounts the story of the epileptic boy who was brought to Jesus by his father.

> Then one of the crowd answered and said, "Teacher,
> I brought You my son, who has a mute spirit. And
> wherever it seizes him, it throws him down; he
> foams at the mouth, gnashes his teeth, and becomes
> rigid. So I spoke to Your disciples, that they should
> cast it out, but they could not." He answered him
> and said, "O faithless generation, how long shall I be
> with you? How long shall I bear with you? Bring
> him to Me." Then they brought him to Him. And

when he saw Him, immediately the spirit convulsed
him, and he fell on the ground and wallowed, foaming at the mouth. So He asked his father, "How long
has this been happening to him?" And he said,
"From childhood. And often he has thrown him
both into the fire and into the water to destroy him.
But if You can do anything, have compassion on us
and help us." Jesus said to him, "If you can believe,
all things are possible to him who believes."
Immediately the father of the child cried out and
said with tears, "Lord, I believe; help my unbelief!"
When Jesus saw that the people came running
together, He rebuked the unclean spirit, saying to it:
"Deaf and dumb spirit, I command you, come out of
him and enter him no more!" Then the spirit cried
out, convulsed him greatly, and came out of him.
And he became as one dead, so that many said, "He
is dead." But Jesus took him by the hand and lifted
him up, and he arose.

—MARK 9:17–27

Here we find the demonic presence causing seizures, but
more interesting still is the action taken by this demon as
Jesus commanded it to come out: The spirit cried out, and as
it left the child, it made him appear dead. As we have seen,
Satan's primary weapon is deception. In this case, either as a
final act of demonic falsehood or as a result of the previous
manifestation, the boy appeared to have died, giving the
appearance of demonic victory. But Jesus saw through this
guise and lifted the boy up. There is no scriptural evidence to
verify that demons by themselves can cause a person's death,
yet this simple deception indicates it is most certainly their

goal. And they might have succeeded in this case if God's power hadn't intervened.

The phenomenon of feigned death has been observed in present-day ministry situations as well. One evening when our team was ministering to a young man who complained of an inability to worship, he fell from his chair and lay on the floor for an hour. Nothing the ministry team said or did had any impact. A few weeks later, the young man returned for ministry, and when Bill began to minister to him, he again fell to the floor. A police officer assisting with the ministry immediately shouted out, "It's a spirit of death!" When the officer proclaimed what the Lord had revealed to him, the young man being ministered to began to take on very real symptoms of death. His body became rigid; all signs of breathing ceased, and it appeared the blood in his limbs had begun to settle. Although this was disturbing, the team stood on the authority of God's Word and continued to minister. Ultimately, the young man was loosed from this spirit of death and received freedom from demonic oppression. He later became a worship leader in a local church. This example doesn't prove whether or not a demon can actually cause death, but it does make clear that they can certainly mimic the appearance of death.

DEMONIC ACTIVITIES ON THE EARTH TODAY

We must remember that demons act in accordance with their evil nature, the purpose of which is theft, death, and destruction. They will operate in any way that furthers those goals. The Bible is the most important source of information regarding demons' actions. Many of the manifestations the Word describes have been seen in the course of modern-day ministry. Current ministry examples convince us that the demonic world is still alive and well and also provide insight into other areas where the demonic is active, even if those areas are not be explicitly stated in Scripture.

On one occasion, Bill met with a young man of college age who was under the influence of a demonic entity that caused him to act like a werewolf. The young man would actually go outside at night and howl at the moon, and the hair on his body had begun to grow extraordinarily long. He also displayed unusual knowledge of a tragic event: When several Russian cosmonauts died in space, this young man described in intricate detail exactly what had caused their death and the condition of their bodies—before they could be recovered. When the bodies were recovered, the young man's information proved accurate. When asked how he had known, the young man replied, "I went out there." This story indicates that demons assist individuals in the practice known as astral projection.

Another occasion highlighted demonic supernatural strength. During this encounter, Bill, who is six feet tall and weighed approximately two hundred fifty pounds, was ministering to a woman who was five feet two and weighed about one hundred thirty pounds. Both were sitting in folding chairs directly across from each other. While Bill was praying for her, the woman slid her foot under the metal bar between the front legs of Bill's folding chair, and with a flip of her foot, Bill suddenly found himself flying across the room and into the wall. This action was performed with enough force that the plastic feet from the end of the folding chair legs remained on the floor. Obviously, this display of supernatural strength was intended to harm Bill, but he remained completely uninjured.

The following summary provides a partial list of other things demons do, as identified by God's Word:

1. They speak (Matthew 8:29).
2. They lie (John 8:44).
3. They argue or question (Matthew 8:29–31).
4. They have supernatural strength (Mark 5:3).
5. They cause violence (Matthew 8:28).
6. They cause sickness and disease (Luke 13:11; Mark 9:20).
7. They control bodily functions (Mark 9:20–22).
8. They have recognition (Matthew 8:29).
9. They know their end (Matthew 8:29).
10. They may possess things or creatures other than humans (Matthew 8:32).
11. They intend to cause death and destruction (Matthew 8:32).
12. They cause self-mutilation (Mark 5:5).
13. They have names (Mark 5:9).
14. They cause muteness and blindness (Matthew 12:22).
15. They cause foaming at the mouth (Mark 9:18).
16. They cause the appearance of death (Mark 9:26).

This list is important in helping us understand that demons act and function as intelligent beings. If we as believers are going to perform the wonders Jesus did, we must be prepared to see the spiritual activities He saw.

Who Can Be Affected by the Demonic?

S ince the primary purpose of the demonic world is to steal, kill, and destroy, the next logical question is, "Who is the primary target of its attack?" Over the years, discussion about demons has raged in the Christian community, but no definitive answer has been reached as to whom can be affected or afflicted by them, especially since their hostile takeovers are frequently denoted by the word *possessed*. Before we discuss how a demon can influence an individual and what makes an individual susceptible to that influence, let's examine the scriptural basis for *possession* and *oppression*.

POSSESSED OR OPPRESSED?

The English word *possessed* implies absolute ownership or control (in this case, of the spirit, soul, and flesh)—so it is difficult to believe a Christian could be possessed by a demon. At the same time, evidence abounds, much of it confirmed by Scripture, that Christians can be demonically influenced. Every time the Greek word *daimonizomai*, translated "possessed," occurs in the New Testament, it refers to the demonic realm (with two notable exceptions—Acts 8:7 and 16:16—where *echo* is used, meaning "to hold"). Although *daimonizomai* is usually translated as "possessed," the actual definition is "to be exercised by a demon—have a (be vexed with, be possessed with) devil(s)." It can also indicate being demonized, annoyed, troubled, or tormented.[1]

Christians, by definition, are owned by Jesus Christ; in other words, they may be disturbed, harassed, and certainly annoyed or plagued by demonic influence, but not owned or possessed.

For clarity, this book will use the terms *possessed* and *oppressed* to delineate the influence a demon can have over an individual. While *possession* implies total, absolute control by the possessor, *oppression* implies harassment, intimidation, and manipulation. Unfortunately, believers can succumb to oppression to such a degree that it can be difficult to distinguish between oppression and possession.

CAN NONBELIEVERS HAVE DEMONS?

The answer is yes. If individuals haven't accepted Jesus' redemption, they are subject to the ruler of this world; therefore, nonbelievers clearly can be oppressed or possessed by demons. Several Scriptures prove this; Mark 7:24–30 is the most clear:

> From there He arose and went to the region of Tyre and Sidon. And He entered a house and wanted no one to know it, but He could not be hidden. For a woman whose young daughter had an unclean spirit heard about Him, and she came and fell at His feet. The woman was a Greek, a Syro-Phoenician by birth, and she kept asking Him to cast the demon out of her daughter. But Jesus said to her, "Let the children be filled first, for it is not good to take the children's

bread and throw it to the little dogs." And she answered and said to Him, "Yes, Lord, yet even the little dogs under the table eat from the children's crumbs." Then He said to her, "For this saying go your way; the demon has gone out of your daughter." And when she had come to her house, she found the demon gone out, and her daughter lying on the bed.

This woman was Greek, a Syro-Phoenician Gentile. Her daughter had a demon (an unclean spirit), which she was beseeching Jesus to "cast out." Since neither she nor her daughter was a covenant-keeping Jew, Jesus tells her that the deliverance she requests is the "children's bread." Yet, because she put her faith in Him, the child was set free.[2] This passage establishes two significant points: (1) Nonbelievers can have demons, and (2) Jesus has authority even in the life of the nonbeliever.

This passage also suggests that nonbelievers typically are not the ones to whom deliverance is offered. In this context, we see that even though Jesus' role was to minister first to the Jewish people, He will also extend His touch to all humankind. However, deliverance is not the first step— acknowledging our faith in Christ is. The woman's statement indicates that she places her trust in Jesus, that He is sufficient even for her, and only after her declaration of faith is Jesus willing to grant her request (notice Jesus responds, "For this saying . . ."). As will be developed in a later chapter, it is very important for the one receiving ministry to believe in Jesus and His authority. Otherwise, casting out demons can potentially do more harm than good.

CAN CHRISTIANS BE CONTROLLED BY DEMONS?

Ephesians 4:30 clearly shows that when someone's life has been turned over to Christ, that person has been sealed for the day of redemption. But it is important that we understand just what part of us has been sealed.

> Now He who establishes us with you in Christ and has anointed us is God, who also has sealed us and given us the Spirit in our hearts as a guarantee.
> —2 CORINTHIANS 1:21–22

As this verse indicates, the heart, or spirit, of a person is sealed for the day of redemption and is the dwelling place of the Holy Spirit. The Holy Spirit and a demonic spirit cannot occupy the same space. However, the Holy Spirit inhabits only the heart, or spirit, of a believer and not the mind or flesh. Paul writes that our whole being needs to be sanctified:

> Now may the God of peace Himself sanctify you completely; and may your whole spirit, soul, and body be preserved blameless at the coming of our Lord Jesus Christ.
> —1 THESSALONIANS 5:23

Nowhere does Scripture indicate that our mind and flesh are sealed as our spirit is sealed. In fact, it is just the opposite (see Romans 7:15–25). So, these two areas—the mind and flesh—are battlegrounds, and warfare is continually conducted to determine who, or what, will rule—the divine will of God or the human will of the soul. As long as we continue to submit our mind and flesh to the Spirit's rule, they are outside demonic jurisdiction; nonetheless, as contested ground, they may become minefields that our adversary can operate in.

So we must be careful to keep our mind and flesh in the ways of the Lord and to focus steadfastly on Him. Paul counsels that nothing good dwells in our flesh (Romans 7:18) and that we should not allow the flesh to fulfill its lusts (Romans 13:14). Left to its own devices, the flesh is not subject to the Holy Spirit, and we must align it with the Spirit's will daily.

Since Paul also admonishes us not to be conformed to this world but transformed by the renewing of our minds (Romans 12:2) and that the carnal mind is at enmity with God (Romans 8:7), evidently putting on the mind of Christ is a battle (Philippians 2:5). If we do not maintain the freshness of this divine relationship through communion in prayer and Scripture, the enemy may temporarily, and in a limited fashion, take "possession" of our flesh or mind. However, he cannot do so without our knowingly or unknowingly giving consent. Knowing consent entails willful rebellion and sin, choosing to walk under the control of our soul rather than the Spirit's leading. Unknowing consent means failing to disallow our fleshly lusts or to conscientiously pursue the renewing of our mind, even though we are not purposefully meaning to rebel.

We can conclude, then, that Christians can have anything they choose or consent (knowingly or unknowingly) to have; consequently, Christians can have demons. It is biblically sound to say that believers can be oppressed, tormented, or hindered but not totally possessed by demons; however, depending on how much authority and control they have relinquished to the enemy, believers may appear to be possessed. For example, let's again examine the story of the woman in Luke 13:

And behold, there was a woman who had a spirit of
infirmity eighteen years, and was bent over and
could in no way raise herself up. But when Jesus saw
her, He called her to Him and said to her, "Woman,
you are loosed from your infirmity." And He laid His
hands on her, and immediately she was made
straight, and glorified God. But the ruler of the syna-
gogue answered with indignation, because Jesus had
healed on the Sabbath; and he said to the crowd,
"There are six days on which men ought to work;
therefore come and be healed on them, and not on
the Sabbath day." The Lord then answered him and
said, "Hypocrite! Does not each one of you on the
Sabbath loose his ox or donkey from the stall, and
lead it away to water it? So ought not this woman,
being a daughter of Abraham, whom Satan has
bound—think of it—for eighteen years, be loosed
from this bond on the Sabbath?" And when he said
these things, all His adversaries were put to shame;
and all the multitude rejoiced for all the glorious
things that were done by Him.

—LUKE 13:11–17

The apostle Paul states, "Therefore know that only those
who are of faith are sons of Abraham" (Galatians 3:7); that is,
if you are a believer as Abraham was, you are a son or daughter of Abraham. Therefore, the woman mentioned in Luke 13
must be a person of faith because she is called by Jesus
Himself a "daughter of Abraham." She keeps the covenant in
faith and is a believer in the pre-Christian sense. She had a
spirit of infirmity and was, in Jesus' own words, one "whom
Satan has bound . . . for eighteen years"—a reference not just

to this woman's sickness. Though not possessed by a demonic entity, the woman in this story was clearly oppressed and
suffering acutely from this spirit of infirmity, whether it
afflicted her anatomy or just loitered around to vandalize her
life. Either way, she wanted to be free. If this covenant-keeping daughter of Abraham could host a spirit of infirmity for
eighteen years, couldn't any believer be a target of demons?

Jesus didn't haltingly protest, "Wait, you're a believer; you
can't have a demon." No, instead He declared freedom, deliverance, and healing. First, He proclaimed her to be loosed from
the spirit of infirmity, and then He laid His hands upon her and
she was healed. In today's society, it is not uncommon to see
occult activity paraded before us, either via the evening news
or through demands for equal *religious* freedom. Satanism,
witchcraft, Wicca, and other occult enterprises are active and
unashamed to be identified. Many unbelievers are heavily
oppressed by these and other satanic groups or influences, and
some have wholly surrendered to them. The impact of demonic oppression is straightforward and easily discernible in some
cases, but it also manifests in more devious, insidious ways
through public recognition of these trends. Make no mistake:
Though not publicly stated, groups rooted in the demonic are
determined to destroy the Church and tear down individual
believers, for this is Satan's avowed agenda.

The men from the tombs in Matthew 8 evidence this type
of covert attack against believers. Verse 28 describes these
demon-possessed men as so fierce that no one could pass by
that way. Another biblical example of the enemy's intent to
destroy God's people is when King Saul was demonically
influenced to throw his spear at David to kill him (1 Samuel
18:10–11). The intention of demonic forces, even though
they may be operating through unbelievers ignorant of their

devices, is to harm, hinder, and halt Christ's followers.

One Halloween several years ago, a well-known revelatory minister was staying in Bill's home. The entire family had retired for the night, and everything seemed to be quiet until Michael was awakened around 1:00 a.m. by his mother pounding at the bedroom door. In a panic, she explained that Bill, his father, had awakened in a state of near suffocation—he was still struggling to breathe. Michael immediately went to the bedroom where the revelatory friend was staying, but before he could even lift his hand to knock, the door opened, and the guest, awake and fully dressed, said, "I've already taken care of the witches; now let's see about your dad." He hastened across the hall and prayed for Bill, who was instantly able to breathe freely again. Later, the guest explained that the Lord had woken him and shown him that a group of witches was praying for Bill's death. He had gone in the spirit (similar to what Obadiah described Elijah doing in 1 Kings 18) and come against them, exercising God's authority over the demonic realm. He knew that when he prayed for Bill, the healing would come. We have never forgotten this incident, and anytime since when we're under demonic attack, it reminds us that God already knows the situation and has already provided the means for us to overcome.

While believers continue to debate whether they can be possessed or just oppressed, God's Word says that our adversary, the devil, is a cunning and wily foe. We must not allow him access through any chink in our armor.

tHE REmEDY:

Exercising God's Authority in Your Life

In the first section, we examined who the enemy is and what he can do. To stop there would give Satan unnecessary glory. It is essential that we now explore how to thwart his plans.

Efforts to stand up to the enemy are usually called *spiritual warfare*, while the specific ministry employed to free an individual from the enemy is termed *deliverance*. The primary topic of this book is the ministry of deliverance.

This section is not designed to offer a formula or procedure for ministering to an individual but to give basic insight into the elements necessary to receive freedom and to help others walk in that freedom. This section is titled "The Remedy" because it addresses how an individual can overcome or "remedy" the demonic attack that has targeted him or her for destruction.

Breaking free from demonic attack isn't particularly easy. It requires work, understanding, and, most importantly, a solid foundation in God's Word. The scriptural principles we discuss here are not intended as a guidebook for dealing with specific problems, but they focus on a broad foundation of biblical principles which will help an individual gain spiritual freedom, regardless of the problem. Whether the issue is satanism, witchcraft, occultism, drugs, alcohol, or anything else that disrupts proper godly and balanced behavior, the following principles will lay a basic foundation for freedom from demonic attacks on believers.

Confession, Repentance, and Forgiveness

Regardless of the type of demonic attack a person is facing, it is happening because the person has been opened to it, either knowingly or unknowingly. In order for a person to experience true freedom from demonic oppression, the root cause must be identified and addressed. If a person is experiencing a great deal of oppression that just won't let up, somewhere an open door has given the enemy a foothold in that individual's life. The initial step in deliverance ministry is to deal with sin and disobedience; however, it is very important to remember that not all oppression a person faces is the result of sin. Some oppression occurs because, like a disease, it literally runs in the family. Certain demonic influences can be passed down through the bloodlines. Traumatic events experienced as a child can also open the door to demonic activity. Confession, repentance, and forgiveness each has a vital role to play in preparing the way for a person's freedom, no matter the type or intensity of oppression.

CONFESSION

Confession is an integral part of every believer's daily walk from the outset of his or her relationship with Jesus Christ.

The Word is clear that confession is crucial to our salvation experience: We must *confess* with our mouth and believe in our heart in order to be saved (Romans 10:9). To put it simply, confession is an act of verbal acknowledgment that brings us into agreement or covenant with God. This element of our Christian walk is so significant that Jesus Himself declares that if we confess Him before men, He will confess us before God. Conversely, if we deny Him before men, He will deny us before God (Matthew 10:33).

Just as confession is significant in receiving salvation, it is also extremely significant in gaining freedom from demonic oppression. 1 John 1:9 validates this:

> If we confess our sins, He is faithful and just to forgive us our sins and to cleanse us from all unrighteousness.

In order to find freedom, any opening for demonic attack we have given the enemy in our lives must be closed. Confession is the first step in closing that opening. When we confess, or acknowledge, where we have fallen short, God is faithful not only to forgive us but also to cleanse us. Forgiveness is necessary for our redemption and reconciliation to God, but cleansing slams shut the doors we have opened to the enemy.

Those seeking freedom from demonic assault must be willing to examine their hearts and allow the Lord to reveal any sin that has given the enemy place in their lives. However, merely recognizing that sin exists or has existed in their lives is not enough: They must confess and acknowledge that sin to God. Confession often is a private matter between the individual and God, but in the context of deliverance, it can also involve confession before others.

Confess your trespasses to one another, and pray for
one another, that you may be healed. The effective,
fervent prayer of a righteous [person] avails much.

—JAMES 5:16

Confession before God gives Him access to forgive and
cleanse, but as the preceding Scripture indicates, when we
confess our trespasses to one another, we can be healed and
minister to one another. The Greek word meaning "healing"
in this verse conveys being cured or made whole. Those subjected to demonic attack need restoration; the enemy has
stolen from them. Confessing to trustworthy ministers the
sins that initially caused the oppression can be an effective
step toward freedom and wholeness.

Obviously, such confession requires trust on the part of
the individual making him- or herself vulnerable, as well as
serious responsibility on the part of those hearing such dis-
closure. The rewards of this type of accountability can be
tremendous. Some of the enemy's most preferred and effective tools to keep people in bondage are secrecy and shame.

REPENTANCE

Confession opens the door to healing, but the process cannot
be completed without true repentance. While confession
acknowledges before God (and/or humanity) what the enemy
has used to hold someone captive, repentance ensures by a
combination of word and deed that such ground is not readily
given up again. Confession admits, "I'm guilty; I'm sorry," but
repentance redirects and reforms an individual's set course.

Now I rejoice, not that you were made sorry, but
that your sorrow led to repentance. For you were

made sorry in a godly manner, that you might suffer
loss from us in nothing.

—2 CORINTHIANS 7:9

Confession and repentance lead to change, and change
makes certain that freedom is received and maintained. If
confession and repentance are not consistently practiced, the
freedom initially gained may be lost later, the person quickly
returning to bondage.

Repentance compels change in attitude and behavior; it
demands determination, for once a person has opened the
door to even the smallest sin, the enemy roars in like a flood.
The destructive habits the enemy produces in an individual
can be difficult to break and need persistence, and sometimes
assistance, to overcome. Repentance is only lip service if one
does not consciously work at changing negative habits—and
God certainly is not mocked; He knows when we are not
being honest with Him, when we have no intention of actually changing our destructive behavior.

However, it is important to remember that when a given
habit leads to a certain course of action or set of circumstances,
it does not always mean that a person has returned to bondage.
Rather, it may be a warning sign that he or she must make further effort to maintain freedom. (A more detailed examination
of this topic is found in Chapter Eight.)

FORGIVENESS

Despite our willingness to confess and repent, we might still
encounter certain hindrances to overcoming demonic
attacks. The greatest barrier to freedom, one that is often
overlooked by well-meaning believers, lies in our own unfor-
giving hearts.

Jesus stated unequivocally that if we do not forgive, we cannot be forgiven:

"For if you forgive men their trespasses, your heavenly Father will also forgive you. But if you do not forgive men their trespasses, neither will your Father forgive your trespasses."

—MATTHEW 6:14–15

This principle is recorded not once but multiple times in the New Testament. Given this scriptural framework, possibly the two greatest blocks to receiving God's fullness are unwillingness to forgive oneself and unwillingness to forgive others.

FORGIVING YOURSELF

Sometimes, it can seem holier for us to forgive others but continue to harbor deep unforgiveness toward ourselves. The importance of the commandment to forgive ourselves in the same way we would forgive others is expressed by Jesus Himself when He is questioned about the greatest commandment:

Then one of the scribes came, and having heard them reasoning together, perceiving that He had answered them well, asked Him, "Which is the first commandment of all?" Jesus answered him, "The first of all the commandments is: 'Hear, O Israel, the LORD our God, the LORD is one. And you shall love the LORD your God with all your heart, with all your soul, with all your mind, and with all your strength.' This is the first commandment. And the second, like it, is this: 'You shall love your neighbor

as yourself.' There is no other commandment greater
than these."

—MARK 12:28–31

This passage deals as much with our relationship with
ourselves as it does with our relationship with God and others. Jesus proclaims, "You shall love your neighbor as yourself." In other words, Jesus would not have us value ourselves
any less or experience any less of His love than we value others and know He values them. He loves them, and us, enough
to die on a cross to reconcile all humanity to Himself. We
must forgive our own trespasses if we seek to be truly free
from any demonic toehold in our lives.

So one of the barriers to freedom from demonic oppression is failing to forgive ourselves. This failure often arises
not from unwillingness, but rather from a lack of understanding its necessity. We tend to judge ourselves by a stricter standard than the one by which we judge others. This can seriously hinder our forgiving ourselves. We must not only be
obedient to God's Word, but we must be recipients of His
promises as well. If God is faithful to forgive us, who are we
to do any less?

FORGIVING VERSUS FORGETTING

Since we were created in the image of a forgiving God, we
inherited this forgiving nature in our spiritual DNA. Not only
has the enemy deceived us by masking God's forgiving nature,
but he has gone for the jugular by convincing many believers
that they have not been forgiven because they have not forgotten. Forgiving does not entail forgetting.

Just because we continue to remember our own or another's
sin does not mean we have not forgiven or been forgiven by

God. Forgiveness is a decision, an act of the will; it is not an emotion and has nothing to do with memory. It is that simple.

Satan is a liar (John 8:44). He continually seeks to convince us that we have not forgiven or been forgiven. We must place our trust and faith in God's Word and not in the enemy's lies. It doesn't matter what we've done or what's been done to us because God will forgive *all* sins, except blaspheming the Holy Spirit . . . and someone seeking help to be free from the enemy's hold is extremely unlikely to be guilty of that sin.

The following example illustrates the connection between forgiveness and deliverance. Sadly, a common root cause of demonic oppression is physical and/or sexual abuse endured as a child. Often, the abuse cycle has continued throughout the person's life. In one such case, the team had been ministering to an individual for some time with limited success because the root of the problem had not yet been identified. By Holy Spirit revelation and the gift of discerning of spirits, it was apparent that demonic forces were cast out. However, this individual's life did not seem to improve. During one session, after much gentle, loving discussion, the individual opened up, and all the physical and sexual abuse she had experienced began to surface. When asked how she felt toward her abusers, she conveyed intense dislike bordering on hatred. The counselors then began a lengthy examination of forgiveness, and after a season of prayer, discussion, and communicating the truth from God's Word, the individual finally decided to forgive. That decision was a choice and not a momentary feeling, and it was somewhat effective. Ministry resumed, but there was still limited success, with no evidence of transformation. The individual remained downcast, depressed, and suicidal.

One problem remained—forgiveness was not yet complete. Although the individual had chosen to forgive her abusers, she had not forgiven herself. When the counselors gingerly broached this issue, they encountered staunch resistance. But once the team was able to show that this was a biblical command, it was accepted and acted upon. The results were phenomenal. The woman's countenance was transfigured. An upbeat attitude began to supplant the weary, downcast nature. Depression and suicide, which had haunted her for most of her life, became a thing of the past. As her bitterness died, this individual's life was transformed. Deliverance had been progressing incrementally all along, but the final and lasting transformation came after choosing to forgive others and herself.

Now, this woman certainly did not immediately forget all the wrongs she had endured. In fact, to date, those memories still linger. However, when she recognized that her entrapment lay not in the memories of what had been done to her, which she could not change, but in her heart attitude toward her abusers, which she could change, she found the key to her freedom. Forgiveness did not mean forgetting or restoring relationship with her abusers (which included several family members). It did mean releasing the mental, emotional, and spiritual captivity wrought by bitterness, anger, and hatred and relinquishing the destructive attitudes that had festered since the abuse.

Longing to rewrite the past also hampers forgiving or receiving forgiveness. The past cannot be changed; we can't do anything about it. We may worry about how others perceive it. We may wallow in what would-have-should-have-could-have been. We can even lie about how it really was. But we cannot change it.

Where we have failed God in the past, we must simply

ask Him for forgiveness, believe His Word is true, and recognize that His forgiveness is ours for the taking. We must embrace God's forgiveness . . . despite our memories. Where others have failed us, we must choose to forgive them, believe it is a decision not an emotion, and move on . . . despite our memories.

Simple Beginnings

Unconfessed sin, false repentance, and unforgiveness can keep us in the fire of demonic attack. Freedom begins when we address these areas. Though they may seem elementary to some, it is amazing how quickly we can be led to forget them during hard times. No monumental revelation or vast and glorious theological point serves to improve this formula: The Gospel remains simple and effective despite our best efforts (and those of the enemy) to make it complicated.

Spiritual Authority, Power, and Weapons

C hapter Four focused on the initial steps one can take to find freedom from oppression. This chapter will build on that foundation and will benefit both those seeking freedom and those ministering to them. Ministry cannot be based on a formula; however, the following scriptural foundation can address any kind of spiritual bondage.

God's Word declares that every believer is a minister. In Ephesians 4:12, the role of the fivefold minister is to equip the saints (believers) for the work of the ministry. While not every believer is called to actual deliverance ministry, every believer does have the capability of ministering in the area of deliverance. Our contemporary mind-set considers ministry a full- or part-time job, but scripturally, ministry simply means fulfilling what the Word of God commands. Every believer is not realistically expected to engage in deliverance as a full- or part-time vocation; however, on the other hand, every believer is called, according to God's Word, to engage in the *work of the ministry*. In other words, everything needed to minister deliverance is present in the life of every believer who is willing to make him- or herself available for the Lord to prepare and use. Scripture confirms this in several different places:

"Whatever you ask . . ." (John 16:23)
"If two of you agree . . ." (Matthew 18:19)
"Behold, I give you the authority . . ." (Luke 10:19)

God has given believers authority and power in His name, along with every spiritual weapon necessary to receive and minister freedom. The work of the ministry is not entrusted only to apostles, prophets, evangelists, pastors, or teachers, but *each one* of us—every disciple of Jesus—has a measure of grace according to Christ's gift (Ephesians 4:7).

In addition to equipping the saints for the work of ministry, the role of the fivefold minister is to edify the Body of Christ so that we *all* come into unity, the fullness of our calling, and spiritual maturity (Ephesians 4:12–13). Fivefold ministers may have responsibilities that differ from others, but they don't have special abilities or are any more capable in and of themselves. What sharply distinguishes fivefold ministers is their level of favor with God and humanity and also an understanding of the anointing.

Both anointing and favor are divine gifts that we cannot humanly manufacture. Put simply, anointing reflects the degree of God's power in an individual's life, while God's favor can be demonstrated by the presence of gifts and the ability to minister successfully in specific areas. Favor with people is granted by God and results in a marked difference in how others receive ministry. Favor and anointing afford true fivefold and vocational ministers greater effectiveness in ministering and increase their spiritual impact and scope.

AUTHORITY

Believers can accomplish the acts described in God's Word only with God's authority. Though we face an enemy who is strong and powerful, every believer has been given authority over him. The primary problem is most believers' failure to recognize the authority available to them.

John 14:12 provides the single greatest grant of authority found in the New Testament:

> "Most assuredly, I say to you, he who believes in Me, the works that I do he will do also; and greater works than these he will do, because I go to My Father."

This is one of the most remarkable promises in God's Word; however, like most of God's promises, it is conditional. Jesus Himself promises that we can do all the works He did (and even greater works), but we must first believe in Him. These words testify that a tremendous amount of authority has been granted believers. Jesus performed some amazing feats: He turned water into wine, made blind eyes see and deaf ears hear; He cleansed lepers and multiplied loaves and fishes; He healed the sick, raised the dead, and drove out demons. And Jesus said whoever desires to do what He did, and greater works, must believe in Him; they must believe they have authority in Him and then follow His example.

Luke 10:19 also records Jesus' giving believers authority:

> "Behold, I give you the authority to trample on serpents and scorpions, and over all the power of the enemy, and nothing shall by any means hurt you."

Here again, Jesus is granting believers authority over the forces of darkness. Serpents and scorpions denote demons and devils, and believers have been given authority to put them under their feet—not just demons and devils but *all* the power of the enemy. The word *all* doesn't leave out anything.

This authority is powerful and offers tremendous supernatural protection from the enemy's plans. For example, Bill was once ministering to a man skilled in various martial arts. During the course of ministry, this man stood up, took a martial arts posture, and began threatening the ministry team. This was potentially a very dangerous situation. But, wielding his authority in the Lord, Bill ordered the man in Jesus' name to sit and be quiet, and the man immediately went rigid and fell backward onto the floor, where he remained for the rest of the ministry time. Knowing the authority we have in Christ averted the potential danger. Interestingly enough, this individual later became one of Bill's most helpful ministry assistants. When we are walking in divine authority, we are also walking in protection from the enemy. Satan's arsenal is neutralized.

POWER

Authority will not be fully respected unless there is the power to uphold it. The difference between power and authority is found in the classic example of the weight lifter and the policeman. Under the right conditions, both of them can stop a moving vehicle. The weight lifter, if properly trained and conditioned, has enough power to lift the wheels off the ground and prevent the car from moving. On the other hand, though a police officer may be unable to lift even a hundred-pound sack of potatoes, his authority can stop the same vehicle. By simply raising his hand and commanding, "Stop!" the police officer accomplishes the same thing the weight lifter did. He is able to stop the vehicle, not in his own strength, but because the law of the land gives him the right to do so and requires every citizen to obey. The officer's authority is enhanced because he carries a weapon in a holster at his side, and he has an army of police officers back at department headquarters ready to assist him.

God's Word has not granted you authority without the power to enforce and enhance it. Everything created by the Word of God is subject to the Word of God—including Satan and the demonic world. The hosts of Heaven stand waiting to help fight against the enemy, and God's Word specifically gives us the power to fight. Jesus promised in Luke 24:49 that when He ascended to Heaven, He would send the Father's promise, and we would be endued with power from on high. Acts 1:8 also confirms the power available to the believer:

> "But you shall receive power when the Holy Spirit
> has come upon you; and you shall be witnesses to
> Me in Jerusalem, and in all Judea and Samaria, and
> to the end of the earth."

This is the same power Jesus used in His deliverance ministry.

> "And if I cast out demons by Beelzebub, by whom
> do your sons cast them out? Therefore they shall be
> your judges. But if I cast out demons by the Spirit of
> God, surely the kingdom of God has come upon
> you."
> —MATTHEW 12:27–28

Jesus cast out demons by the Spirit of God, with the very same power you have. This power is the Holy Spirit's presence in your life, enabling you to accomplish what you have been given the authority to do.

WEAPONS

The gifts and weapons Jesus gave us work only because the Holy Spirit directly empowers them. To understand their use in ministry, it is important to understand the difference between the weapons and the tools God supplies. Weapons are the implements to convey power, just like the police officer's gun; tools are the methods we use to accomplish what God has given us to do.

This book isn't meant to provide a detailed analysis of the tools available for deliverance ministry, which may include questionnaires, lists of commonly encountered demonic strongholds, interviewing methods, and more. However, weapons are scripturally based and must be used no matter what type of ministry we're doing.

PRAYER

The most powerful and effective weapon available to the believer is prayer. Prayer is not a posture, a position, or an eloquent speech. It is not determined by education or the ability to be heard over a crowd. God speaks your language. No one has to pray in biblical King James English. Prayer does not entail reciting sundry religious clichés or barraging God with instructions. Simply put, prayer means communicating with God in a way that seeks His will in our life or in another's.

Praying with command and authority is an invaluable principle of prayer that is often overlooked. It proclaims the spiritual authority of God's Word and commands demonic forces to honor and obey that authority. Jesus employed this type of prayer nearly every time He freed people from demonic forces. Also, He often prepared for ministry by spending the whole night in the mountains alone in prayer. Then, when the time came to actually touch an individual's life,

Jesus exercised command and authority. Examples of this are numerous throughout the Gospels.

For instance, when Jesus confronted the two demon-possessed men among the tombs in Matthew 8, He simply commanded, "Go," and the demons departed. In Luke 4, again Jesus merely orders obedience, and it is done:

> But Jesus rebuked him, saying, "Be quiet, and come out of him!" And when the demon had thrown him in their midst, it came out of him and did not hurt him.
>
> —LUKE 4:35

Jesus exemplified that, when dealing with the demonic realm on earth, the believer has absolute authority to command obedience.

THE NAME OF JESUS

For the believer, the ability to command the enemy comes through the use of Jesus' name:

> "And whatever you ask in My name, that I will do, that the Father may be glorified in the Son. If you ask anything in My name, I will do it."
>
> —JOHN 14:13–14

If Jesus could say, "Go," and demons departed, then every believer has the ability to command, "Go in the name of Jesus," and see equal results. The name of Jesus is one of the most powerful weapons of our warfare.

Using Jesus' name is powerful. Simply saying "Jesus" doesn't always carry authority—after all, many people invoke His name as a swearword—but we as believers, the servants of

God, carry His authority and don't actually have to speak Jesus' name in order to use it. In ancient times, when a king sent out his servants, they were empowered to act "in the name of the king." This power did not demand the addition of "in the king's name" to their every request, command, or action; rather, the use of the king's name meant that, as his servants, what they did or said on his behalf had the same force and effect as though he himself were present. As Ephesians 4 saints maturing in the ways of the Holy Spirit, all believers have been given authority to use the name of the King of Kings, and what we do or say (as long as we are walking in the Spirit) carries authority. Kings throughout history have sent ambassadors to conduct their business. The King of Kings, being omnipresent and resident within every believer, stands with us whenever we invoke the authority of His name. Our authority to use Jesus' name is inherent in our relationship with the King Himself.

Even though we don't have to verbalize Jesus' name to use it, speaking His name is still very important in ministry and prayer, as Scripture clearly demonstrates. One biblical example is the account of the slave girl in Acts:

> Now it happened, as we went to prayer, that a certain slave girl possessed with a spirit of divination met us, who brought her masters much profit by fortune-telling. This girl followed Paul and us, and cried out, saying, "These men are the servants of the Most High God, who proclaim to us the way of salvation." And this she did for many days. But Paul, greatly annoyed, turned and said to the spirit, "I command you in the name of Jesus Christ to come out of her." And he came out that very hour.
>
> —ACTS 16:16–18

Jesus' name is above every other name, and at His name every knee will bow (Philippians 2:10). So, when we glorify Jesus' name through a walk consistent with His character and nature and when we physically speak His name, we wield a mighty weapon against the forces of darkness.

THE BLOOD OF JESUS

An equally effective weapon of warfare is Christ's blood. Jesus' shed blood is a continual reminder to the enemy that his best-laid plans failed. In the moment he perceived to be his ultimate triumph, the crucifixion of Jesus, Satan met his ultimate defeat. Jesus' innocent blood was spilled as the perfect sacrifice for sin and restored the opportunity for human relationship with God. Each time Jesus' blood is mentioned in the presence of demonic spirits, they are forced to recall the humiliation they suffered when their plans went awry and their doom was sealed. The terror the mere mentioning of Jesus' blood inspires among demonic spirits is heartening; yet, to truly use Jesus' blood effectively as a weapon, we must understand its biblical basis.

> "And they overcame him by the blood of the Lamb and by the word of their testimony, and they did not love their lives to the death."
> —REVELATION 12:11

The blood of the Lamb (Jesus) is a weapon used to overcome the great dragon, Satan, the serpent of old (Revelation 12:9). If Jesus' blood is sufficient to overcome the devil himself, then it definitely is an effective weapon against his demonic forces.

THE WORD OF GOD

One easily overlooked weapon is the direct use of God's Word. Memorization of Scripture is powerful and effective. The Word that proceeds from the mouth of the Lord will accomplish its purpose.

> "So shall My word be that goes forth from My mouth;
> It shall not return to Me void,
> But it shall accomplish what I please,
> And it shall prosper in the thing for which I sent it."
> —ISAIAH 55:11

It is powerful to have someone read from the Word while ministry is taking place. During one ministry session, Bill learned that not only is Scripture an effective weapon when proclaimed boldly against our adversary, but the Bible (as a book) itself can also be useful. While ministering to a young woman, Bill placed his Bible across her hands, which were resting on her knees. When he did, she immediately asked, "Would you take that book off my hands, please?" Recognizing that something unique was taking place, Bill refused and told her that if she wanted it off, she would have to remove it herself. After a few moments of debate, she insisted that she didn't want to remove it because if she did, it would ruin the ministers' faith. Bill, unwilling to give in to this demonic challenge, again refused to remove the Bible. Finally, the young woman (or more particularly, the demonic entity working through her) acceded and said, "Would you move the book, please? It is burning my hands." While the Bible does not identify itself in its book form as an effective weapon, this experience reveals that God's Word, in any form, is formidable.

Anointing Oil

Anointing oil is another potent weapon in ministry, although it is mentioned only briefly in Scripture. Oil, in and of itself, is insignificant, but when it has been prayed over and consecrated to the Lord, it can wreak damage on darkness. Oil represents the Holy Spirit's presence and the anointing. In the Old Testament, it was an integral part of the furnishings of the tabernacle. In Exodus 25:6, it kept the flames of the tabernacle lamps alive and was also used for anointing. In Leviticus 8:10–12, it was used for anointing both the tabernacle and the priest. In the New Testament, anointing with oil is connected with healing ministry and is also a strong weapon in deliverance (itself a form of healing). Perhaps the most famous Scripture outlining the use of anointing oil is James 5:14:

> Is anyone among you sick? Let him call for the elders of the church, and let them pray over him, anointing him with oil in the name of the Lord.

Another passage that indicates Jesus approved the use of anointing oil and probably instructed his disciples in its use is Mark 6:13:

> And they cast out many demons, and anointed with oil many who were sick, and healed them.

While Scripture doesn't specifically connect anointing oil to deliverance ministry, oil has proved beneficial, as the following story demonstrates. In ministering to a young woman who was heavily involved in the occult, and had willingly participated in several human sacrifices, our team ultimately found it difficult to get her to commit to the deliverance process. On a few occasions after ministry began, she actually jumped up and fled the room. Wanting to help her, the ministry team continued to work with her. The final time Bill saw her for ministry, she was sitting at his desk weeping. Bill instructed one of his ministry assistants to put anointing oil on his hand and place it on her head. When he did, she screamed loudly, fell to the floor, and lay there screaming for quite a while. Finally, a particularly strong demonic entity surfaced, caused her to stand, and announced the woman was leaving. Bill's ministry assistant, experimenting with this newfound weapon, reached over and rubbed his oily hand on the doorknob to the only exit from the room. When the woman reached the door, she examined the knob carefully and tried to touch it several times. At last, in desperation, she gingerly gripped the doorknob with a bunch of tissues and escaped the room. Unfortunately, she never returned for further ministry. Although this situation could be viewed as a failure, the lesson learned about the power of anointing oil has been a significant help in setting many others free.

BINDING AND LOOSING

God's Word establishes the principle of binding and loosing as a powerful weapon against demons. Matthew 18:18 outlines this principle:

> "Assuredly, I say to you, whatever you bind on earth will be bound in heaven, and whatever you loose on earth will be loosed in heaven."

In a later chapter, we will discuss the principle of binding and loosing as it relates to spiritual warfare. Demonic entities must be present in the earthly realm to oppress individuals;

because of this, believers can bind these demonic entities and order their activity to cease. Binding the enemy forces him to loose minds or emotions and allows the people under this intense oppression to think for themselves. Scripture and experience attest how crucial this principle is to deliverance ministry . . . and beyond.

In the early days of ministry, before fully understanding how to use this weapon, Bill would frequently request aid from other men in restraining those receiving ministry. This was to keep them from hurting themselves. He learned by experience that this was not the most effective method and that it gave the enemy the opportunity to bring accusations against the ministry. One day while ministering to a young man who was about to get up from his folding chair and attack those ministering to him, Bill declared, "In the name of Jesus, I bind your hands to the sides of that chair." For the rest of the ministry session, the young man could not remove his hands from the chair. He continued trying to get up and actually ran around the room holding the chair against him, but he was unable to release it. It is important to remember here that the demonic entity was controlling the young man's actions, not the young man himself. When the demonic presence was gone, the man was completely free to exercise his will to release the chair.

Binding and loosing is effectual both when commanding demonic entities to depart and when deliverance may not be the appropriate action. Occasionally, individuals may be so oppressed and confused that they can't clearly decide whether they actually want freedom or not. In this circumstance, it would be appropriate to bind the demonic entities from operating and command them to loose the people's minds, allowing the people a respite of peace and rest so the

Lord may act. Binding and loosing can open the door for the
Lord to draw individuals into freedom.

AGREEMENT

The biblical principle of agreement can be an excellent asset in
spiritual warfare. Agreement not only concentrates the delivery
of God's power but actually multiplies its effectiveness.
Unfortunately, believers rarely actually agree. The primary scriptural basis for the principle of agreement is found in Matthew:

> "Again I say to you that if two of you agree on earth
> concerning anything that they ask, it will be done
> for them by My Father in heaven."
> —MATTHEW 18:19

In addition to the virtually unlimited favor God grants as
a result of agreement, His Word states that when two or more
come together in agreement, a tremendous increase in impact
is released. Deuteronomy 32:30 testifies that, when the Lord
is in charge, one can put a thousand to flight and two can put
ten thousand to flight. Spiritual force increases exponentially
when two or more individuals agree. Unfortunately, believers
have not yet tapped in to the full manifestation of this power
because we rarely arrive at actual agreement.

The weapon of agreement is based on being of one
accord. Though believers often express agreement with a particular prayer or proclamation, all too often this is not actually true agreement. Commonly, the group of believers is
mentally *assenting* that something is probably true without
ever really *agreeing* that it is. Even when believers do agree,
they are often violating the biblical principle of *asking* by asking with the wrong motives. Every passage of Scripture must

be taken in context with the rest of God's Word if we are to properly interpret it. In this case, the Word says that, when two agree, they can have whatever they ask, but we must always take note of how and why we ask. James 4:2–3 elucidates this issue:

> You lust and do not have. You murder and covet and cannot obtain. You fight and war. Yet you do not have because you do not ask. You ask and do not receive, because you ask amiss, that you may spend it on your pleasures.

When we link this passage with Matthew 18, we realize our prayers may not be answered not only because we don't ask but also because we are asking amiss. For the agreement and asking principles to function, we must ask according to what God wants rather than what we want. Too often, our prayers are based on our human desires instead of on God's heart. In order to properly utilize the weapon of agreement, we must go beyond a mental assent and find the mind of God for what we are asking. When these principles are applied, agreement will become a powerful weapon in the believer's arsenal.

The Bottom Line

We must be willing to use the weapons God has provided and not be cowed to inaction by fear or expect someone else to do the job we've been called to do. All the authority, power, and weapons—the remedy Jesus won for us—are useless unless we are willing to use them.

The Source
of Power

B elievers must harness a supernatural power to deal with
demons: the Holy Spirit. According to John 14:26, the
Holy Spirit is given as our Teacher in spiritual matters, our
Helper, and our Guide along the path of righteousness. He
becomes the mouthpiece of God the Father, giving us
instructions from God's Word and by that still small voice He
uses to speak directly to our hearts. In John 14:26, Jesus
states that the Holy Spirit will be sent in His name both to
teach us and to bring us into remembrance of what He said.
The Holy Spirit also empowers believers by diverse gifts
given as He chooses. Sometimes described as a second filling
of the Holy Spirit, another aspect of the Holy Spirit's role in a
believer's life is the baptism of the Holy Spirit.

> When the Day of Pentecost had fully come, [Jesus'
> disciples] were all with one accord in one place. And
> suddenly there came a sound from heaven, as of a
> rushing mighty wind, and it filled the whole house
> where they were sitting. Then there appeared to
> them divided tongues, as of fire, and one sat upon
> each of them. And they were all filled with the Holy

Spirit and began to speak with other tongues, as the
Spirit gave them utterance.

—Acts 2:1–4

The filling with the Holy Spirit in Acts 2 is designed to
empower disciples to be witnesses:

"But you shall receive power when the Holy Spirit
has come upon you; and you shall be witnesses to
Me in Jerusalem, and in all Judea and Samaria, and
to the end of the earth."

—Acts 1:8

After they were filled with the Holy Spirit in Acts 2, they
immediately began to exercise power and authority and boldly preach the Gospel. The baptism of the Holy Spirit empowers the believer to be a more effective witness. As will be discussed later in this book (see point six of Chapter Eight,
"How to Stay Free"), the gift of speaking in tongues is an
empowerment and a tremendous tool in the context of deliverance. It can be evidence that a believer has experienced the
baptism of the Holy Spirit, just as it was one sign of this experience on the Day of Pentecost; however, the primary evidence
even on the Day of Pentecost was the empowerment of the
disciples. The gift of tongues should not be overemphasized,
as Scripture is equally clear that this is not the only sign of
having been filled with the Holy Spirit. Acts 19 specifically
shows that prophecy is also a sign of this experience:

And when Paul had laid hands on them, the Holy
Spirit came upon them, and they spoke with tongues
and prophesied.

—Acts 19:6

Many nonbelievers who came into contact with the disciples became empowered believers whose lives were visibly changed. We know that the change in these believers' lives had some visible manifestation because of what Simon says in Acts 8:18:

> And when Simon saw that through the laying on of the apostles' hands the Holy Spirit was given, he offered them money.

The key phrase here is "when Simon saw." Simon saw a change in the lives of these believers—evidence that an impartation had occurred and that they had received the Power spoken of in Acts 1:8.

EVIDENCE OF THE HOLY SPIRIT'S EMPOWERMENT

The term *empowerment* conveys an installation of power, especially legal power or official authority, and can also mean "to equip or to supply with an ability; to enable."[1] Empowerment is essential for successful deliverance ministry.

Official authority is conveyed to the believer in Luke 10:19, when Jesus states, "Behold, I give you the authority." But Jesus also admonishes us, "The Helper, the Holy Spirit, whom the Father will send in My name, He will teach you all things, and bring to your remembrance all things that I said to you" (John 14:26). So, the Holy Spirit teaches us and reminds us of the authority Jesus promised in Luke 10:19 and, according to Acts 1:8, has come that we might have power to be witnesses. So, just what does it mean to be a witness? The answer can be found in Mark 16:15–18:

> And He said to them, "Go into all the world and

preach the gospel to every creature. He who believes
and is baptized will be saved; but he who does not
believe will be condemned. And these signs will follow those who believe: *In My name they will cast out
demons* [emphasis added]; they will speak with new
tongues; they will take up serpents; and if they drink
anything deadly, it will by no means hurt them; they
will lay hands on the sick, and they will recover."

One of the evidences of Holy Spirit empowerment is the
ability to cast out demons in Jesus' name, but the empowerment manifests in other ways as well.

Scripture maintains that the Holy Spirit gives gifts to
believers when He fills them. Among the gifts identified in 1
Corinthians 12 are several that have become essential in deliverance ministry. Two of the more prominent gifts utilized in
deliverance are discerning of spirits and the word of knowledge, which is mentioned in 1 Corinthians 12:8. The gift of
discerning of spirits is helpful both in determining if the problem is, at its core, demonic or carnal and if what is spoken by
the one being ministered to is actually the truth. Words of
knowledge can identify the root cause that allowed the enemy
access in the first place and assist in closing that door.

Other gifts can also be identified as evidence of empowerment. The gift of healings can function side by side with
the casting out of demons, as has already been discussed. A
word of wisdom can provide valuable insight as to when and
how to proceed with ministry. The gift of faith obviously can
have significant impact. If a person can say, without doubt, to
the mountain, "Be removed," and it will be done (Mark
11:23), then he or she can certainly say to demons, "Leave,"
and they will. Each of these gifts, in general or specifically in

the context of deliverance ministry, shows the empowering role the Holy Spirit plays in our lives.

CONCLUSION

Without question, every individual receives the Holy Spirit at the moment of salvation; Scripture is clear that one cannot experience the wonder of salvation without the Holy Spirit's presence. However, Scripture is equally clear that the Holy Spirit's work doesn't stop there: He desires to empower all believers and to make them more effective witnesses of God. When believers accept the baptism of the Holy Spirit, their lives will be changed. There will be a visible difference that other believers and even nonbelievers will be able to see; this may or may not include speaking in tongues.

Individuals engaging in deliverance ministry would be wise to exert great care in choosing fellow ministry workers: Merely being a believer is not generally a sufficient qualification for this ministry; being an empowered believer is preferable. However, God does honor our faith, and all believers (even without a full, mature understanding of their Power source) are ministers and can be used in unexpected ways and circumstances by God.

Practical Suggestions on Deliverance

The first two sections of this book have dealt with foundational elements of deliverance ministry. This final section offers practical suggestions for ministering to others: preparing a person to receive ministry, remaining free after ministry, and understanding limitations in ministry. Simply knowing one's enemy and oneself will enable an individual to minister to others, but these practical suggestions will make that ministry much easier and more effective. It is important that deliverance ministers not only understand the principles already discussed but also know how to practically help others prepare to be delivered.

Engaging
in Ministry

People must be prepared in advance to receive deliverance ministry, but the person ministering must also be prepared for whatever could take place. Romans 12:10–12, though not specifically referring to deliverance ministry, serves as a code of conduct deliverance ministers might take to heart.

> Be kindly affectionate to one another with brotherly love, in honor giving preference to one another; not lagging in diligence, fervent in spirit, serving the Lord; rejoicing in hope, patient in tribulation, continuing steadfastly in prayer.

A sincere desire to see others set free can help overcome many of the difficulties associated with this ministry. The full strata of society is represented in the variety of those needing deliverance. The only thing they all have in common is that some open door in their life has allowed the enemy to gain a foothold. Quite frequently, this is uncomfortable for them to discuss because habits of mind and/or body can make them feel embarrassed or humiliated. A deliverance minister must maintain a tactful, compassionate, yet intrepid approach to those being

ministered to, even though the minister will frequently be confronted with issues that would cause many believers to want to
run and hide rather than stand and fight. Only unconditional
love can enable the minister to overcome such obstacles.

In addition, the deliverance minister must be willing to
give preference to those in need of ministry. Giving preference
doesn't mean the minister should bow down to every demand
of those in need; rather, it means not allowing the minister's
own preconceived notions of a person's character to cause a
presumptuous judgment about the degree of deliverance that
person needs. When we prefer others, we place their needs
ahead of our own and so do not allow any need for recognition on our part outweigh the other individual's need to
receive what God is doing. Otherwise, we may assume others
need deliverance merely because their personality type differs
from or conflicts with our own or because their life habits
have created strongholds that need to be overcome (this latter
point will be discussed later in this chapter). Through unconditional love and preferring others, the deliverance minister
will also ensure that the proper time is taken to prepare the
recipient to receive, instead of demanding he or she simply
accept what the minister intends to do.

"Not lagging in diligence, fervent in spirit, serving the
Lord" (Romans 12:11) are among the most challenging elements of this code of conduct. Just because the minister
understands his or her own authority, power, and weapons
does not ensure that every case will be an open-and-shut
matter. The bottom line is that this service may require one
to stand steadfastly and, having done all, simply to continue
to stand (Ephesians 6:13).

It takes commitment to search for the open door, to keep
on teaching the person to prepare to receive, to continue

encouraging the person to forgive, and to persist in reaching out, even if the circumstances seem to offer no hope for success. Deliverance ministers must persevere, even in the face of rejection, for not everyone who needs this ministry accepts it with open arms; in fact, the deliverance minister can at times face open hostility.

Also, deliverance ministers must remember that a lack of immediate results does not equal failure. God's Word has always provided hope for the hopeless, and the trials and tribulations of deliverance ministry are merely the testing ground to mature everyone involved. Finally, those embarking on this ministry must be fully and absolutely committed to prayer, both as an element of preparation and as the primary weapon employed *to set the captives free.*

DEMON STRONGMAN VERSUS CARNAL STRONGHOLD

Deliverance ministers must also discipline themselves to resist looking for a demon under every rock. One mistake made by those new to this ministry is attributing every problem to the demonic. In fact, both the deliverance minister and the individual who has come for help should begin *without* presuming deliverance is the answer. The need for deliverance should be suspected only after the normal channels of prayer, repentance, application of the Word, and other spiritual disciplines have been applied without a marked victory.

Also, as has already been stated, the person receiving ministry must truly want to be free, no matter what way of life he or she has to give up or change. Sin is still sin and has consequences. There is a clear difference between habitual sin that has established a carnal stronghold and an uncontrollable manifestation of a demonic strongman who has set up residence in or around an individual. When sin has reached the level where it is engaged in virtually without thought, it will open the door to demonic activity. But the individual's problem is not always a demon; it could be a stronghold.

A stronghold is defined as an area in an individual's life that has been surrendered to habitual sin. This can be a significant issue, since the minister has no authority over another individual's life. When a demon is the problem, the deliverance minister has absolute authority in Christ. But when the problem actually exists in the individual's soul—that is, the mind, will, and emotions—a different approach is called for. When an individual's will is involved, the Holy Spirit will not violate that will, and He will not allow the minister to override it, either. Instead, the individual receiving ministry must acknowledge entrenched sin and be taught to overcome it.

When the person has clearly repented and taken the necessary steps to overcome his or her own carnal nature without success, we can then suspect demonic activity is operating. Too often, deliverance ministers feel they have failed because they have improperly tried to cast out the flesh, when the flesh should be disciplined, crucified, and overcome.

TEACHING THOSE IN NEED TO AID IN THEIR OWN DELIVERANCE

The deliverance minister must be a teacher as well. (We are not suggesting that every believer will occupy the office of the teacher mentioned in Ephesians 4; we are simply pointing out that every believer has a responsibility to communicate the basic elements of the Gospel and that there is scriptural support for freedom from demonic harassment.) God's Word anticipates that those who come to Christ will share what they have learned with those around them. This expectation is no different for deliverance ministry. The one offering prayer and ministry has an understanding of how the demonic realm operates and how to travel the road to freedom that the person in need does not. Never overlook the importance of conveying this information as a prelude to actual ministry.

1. *Hate sin.* To be set free from demonic oppression, individuals must truly learn to hate sin. When we are born again, we acquire an aversion to sin via our God-given conscience, but we must also learn to actively repudiate sin, no matter how inconsequential it may seem.

2. *Desire complete freedom.* All too often people seeking deliverance ministry desire to be set free from a specific problem but not to be *free indeed.* Expressed another way, many people want to be free only from the problems caused by the demonic oppression, while hanging on to the potential benefits. To truly obtain total freedom, one must sincerely desire complete deliverance from all demonic activity. 1 Corinthians 5:6 uses the analogy of leaven in a loaf of bread. To paraphrase this verse, one could say that without complete freedom from demonic attack, everything just comes back.

3. *Reject the demonic.* Another common misconception among those seeking help is that they cannot get free by calling on God themselves. Taking authority as a believer and rejecting and renouncing the sin in one's own life are some of the first steps toward freedom. In some cases, this is all that is necessary. Even when prayer and ministry are needed, self-examination, evaluation, and subsequent action are fundamental. Remember, God's Word doesn't give authority only to pastors, evangelists, leaders, and those who minister deliverance, but it also gives authority to *you.* Every believer has the

authority in Christ to subdue the enemy. At the very least, those in need of deliverance should be taught the principle of binding and loosing found in Matthew 18:18.

4. *Get rid of reminders.* It is important for those who have been involved in overt demonic activity to rid themselves and their surroundings of any reminder of that involvement. While this may be taken to an extreme (such as believing no Christian should have any object shaped like a frog, resembling a frog, or depicting a frog), it is better to take this removal to an extreme than to ignore it altogether. All objects used in occult practices or sinful activity should be disposed of. Scripture confirms that such objects can be the focal point for demonic attack, and the enemy loves using these things to sow doubts about an individual's ability to overcome a particular sinful pattern.

5. *Prayer and fasting.* Anyone coming for ministry should understand the biblical principles of prayer and fasting and their accompanying power. An individual's preparation to receive ministry should be covered in prayer and instruction in the power incurred by fasting—a power that can multiply exponentially. When we exercise our will and overcome our flesh by denying it, we establish within ourselves a firm foundation for ministry. Self-denial through fasting demands that we elevate God's Word over our own desires and allow our spirit to take its rightful position of authority over our soul and flesh. Jesus Himself advised that some demonic spirits come out only through prayer and fasting (Matthew 17:21). Prayer as communication with the Holy Spirit enables both the individual ministering and the individual receiving ministry to share with the Father their concerns, their desires, and their questions, in anticipation of His responses. Fasting prepares us to hear God's voice more accurately during min-

istry and so be better prepared to give and receive.

As a side note, during ministry, those being ministered to should receive; it is not the time they should engage actively in prayer but allow the Holy Spirit to minister to them through the other believers present.

6. *Honesty.* People receiving ministry should be encouraged to be completely honest and hold nothing back. For this to be beneficial, the person ministering must be prepared for whatever he or she may hear. It is not required, nor in most cases even desirable, for those receiving ministry to share every detail of their lives. The Lord already knows these details: "God, You know my foolishness, / And my sins are not hidden from You" (Psalm 69:5). Nevertheless, those undergoing deliverance must be willing to acknowledge the sin that has allowed the enemy's onslaught so that they can find freedom. Often, one of the enemy's most successful tactics is to convince us that the sin we hide cannot hurt us. In truth, hiding sin empowers it against us. Never forget who our enemy is and what his tools are. He is a master of deception and is not to be believed. The very nature of this ministry requires that we support a person's openness and honesty, but at the same time, we need to be wary of his or her truthfulness during the course of ministry itself. Since demons can and do speak through people, we must discern whether we are listening to the enemy or to the individual actually receiving ministry.

The following example shows how the enemy tries to deceive in any way he can. On this occasion, the demonic entity stated that it wouldn't leave and that Bill had no authority to make it leave. Bill firmly told it that the Word of God gave him authority over demons, so it had to leave. At this point, in a high-pitched voice, Bill was told, "I'm gone." Unfortunately, this was not true, as was discerned both spiritually by the ministry team and physically by the nature of the statement itself (had the demon truly been gone, the individual would have said, "*It's* gone," instead of saying, "*I'm* gone"). After some additional ministry, the demonic entity left, and the individual was truly set free. This may seem humorous on the surface; however, it clearly illustrates that no matter how much you expect an individual to be honest with you, not every word uttered during a session can be trusted as truth.

7. *Physical manifestations/reactions.* Both those needing ministry and those ministering should be prepared for physical manifestations and/or reactions during the course of ministry. The Greek word for spirit is *pneuma*, which means "breath," and many demonic spirits are expelled in a breathy manner, such as coughing, burping, sighing, yawning, screaming, weeping, vomiting, etc. Neither the individual nor those ministering should be surprised or embarrassed by these manifestations. There could be other physical reactions as well, but these needn't cause undue alarm, either. It's also possible that successful deliverance ministry won't have any physical reaction whatsoever.

CONCLUSION

Engaging in deliverance ministry can be challenging and demanding. It requires a greater level of preparation than those receiving ministry. The deliverance minister's code of conduct is vital in this preparation. By focusing on God's Word, we can more easily overcome the enemy's attempts to distract us with negative manifestations.

Regarding demonic attempts to stop or at least frustrate deliverance ministry, it would appear the forces of darkness have taken to heart the familiar saying, "If you can't beat them, join them." Because of the natural tendency of someone new to this ministry to think demons are the cause of every difficulty, the enemy has successfully burned out many anointed ministers. By encouraging deliverance ministers to see a demon under every rock, the enemy attempts to overwhelm them and cause them to "grow weary in doing good" (2 Thessalonians 3:13).

Finally, the importance of teaching those who come for ministry cannot be emphasized enough: Individuals must have a basic understanding of what is about to take place and a familiarity with God's Word. The steps identified in this chapter help us prepare to engage in effective ministry and avoid any overconfidence in our own strength, which leads to failure.

How to Stay Free

Merely delivering an individual from demonic oppression is not enough. For deliverance ministry to be truly successful, ministers must also ensure that person understands what it takes to remain free. This is why deliverance ministry is not recommended for unbelievers. For those receiving ministry, keeping their deliverance is as important as getting it—perhaps even more important.

Jesus Himself explained the damage involved when a person does not maintain deliverance:

> "When an unclean spirit goes out of a man, he goes
> through dry places, seeking rest; and finding none, he
> says, 'I will return to my house from which I came.' And
> when he comes, he finds it swept and put in order. Then
> he goes and takes with him seven other spirits more
> wicked than himself, and they enter and dwell there;
> and the last state of that man is worse than the first."
>
> —LUKE 11:24–26

Indisputably, if deliverance is not maintained, the situation becomes worse than before. Unclean spirits, or demons, are not content to leave on command and never return. Instead, while they may obey the believer's command, they remain ready and anxious to return to their former abode and continue their destructive work.

Teaching individuals how to maintain their freedom is not optional. Deliverance ministers cannot afford to bypass this training. Such training is, however, quite difficult for unsaved people to utilize. If people don't comprehend even the basic principles of salvation, they will probably not comprehend the spiritual disciplines they must follow to maintain their freedom, nor be able to apply them. In fact, when control of one's life has not been transferred from the god of this world to the God of the universe, a demonic oppressor's return is extremely likely.

How does a person maintain freedom after deliverance? By obeying God's Word. The following list of biblical life principles is far from exhaustive but should be practiced by every person who has received deliverance.

1. *Yield every area of your life to the lordship of Christ.* This is a basic element of every Christian's life, yet it is surprising how many people do not understand it. Salvation recognizes Christ as Savior, but it is much more difficult for us to recognize Him as Lord. Believing on His name for salvation does not mean we're also bowing to His lordship. In fact, the book of Matthew points out that there will be those who call Him Lord but do not know Him:

> "Not everyone who says to me, 'Lord, Lord,' shall enter the kingdom of heaven, but he who does the will of My Father in heaven. Many will say to Me in that day, 'Lord, Lord, have we not prophesied in

Your name, cast out demons in Your name, and done many wonders in Your name?' And then I will declare to them, 'I never knew you; depart from Me, you who practice lawlessness!'"

—Matthew 7:21–23

To be completely and consistently free from demonic oppression, one must yield control to Christ. Yielding complete control of one's life is not easy, but we must strive to walk in this surrender daily. Also, we must confess immediately when we fail. 1 John 1:9 affirms that when we confess our sins, He is faithful and just to forgive us and to cleanse us from all unrighteousness.

2. *Be continuously filled with the Holy Spirit.* The Holy Spirit is the source of believers' power, and when we continually seek His infilling, we are strengthened. According to Paul, when we daily put to death the deeds of the flesh and are led by the Spirit, we have life (Romans 8:6). The devil's role is to steal, kill, and destroy. When we put to death the works of our flesh and live by the Spirit, we do not permit theft, death, and destruction to abide in us.

3. *Live by the Word of God.* Living by God's Word doesn't mean we simply believe it's true; it means we put it into practice. Jesus exemplified living by God's Word when Satan tempted Him in the wilderness. Jesus was tempted three times, and each time He responded, "It is written . . ." (Matthew 4:4, 7, 10). Jesus' statements were not merely a rote recitation of the memorized Word; they were life. They were the answer to the situation that he faced. He demonstrated to the enemy, and to us, that He not only knew God's Word but lived by it.

4. *Put on the whole armor of God.* The armor of God is our "uniform" of spiritual warfare, our "battle fatigues." This is true

for both those ministering deliverance and those receiving and walking out their freedom. Ephesians 6:10–18 outlines the armor of God, which serves as protection and offensive positioning. The breastplate of righteousness and the shield of faith protect a soldier, while the sword of the Spirit can be an offensive weapon that reaches beyond the soldier's normal sphere of influence. However, donning the armor of God daily without walking in godly character is ineffectual. These are weapons of the Spirit, and so, to bear these arms victoriously, one must walk in the Spirit.

5. *Cultivate a renewed mind.* Those who wish to live according to the Spirit set their minds on the things of the Spirit because being carnally minded brings death (Romans 8:5–7). Paul tells us not to be conformed to the image of this world but transformed by the renewing of our minds (Romans 12:2). The renewal of our minds is not a onetime prayer or deliverance but a daily effort to fix our minds on godly, not worldly, pursuits.

6. *Pray in the Spirit.* Paul states that when one prays in a tongue, it is his or her spirit that prays (1 Corinthians 14:14) and speaks not to humanity but to God.

> For he who speaks in a tongue does not speak to men but to God, for no one understands him; however, in the spirit he speaks mysteries.
>
> —1 CORINTHIANS 14:2

Also, according to 1 Corinthians 2:10, it is the Holy Spirit who searches out the deep things, who brings understanding to the mysteries spoken when one prays in tongues. Praying in tongues enables us to speak mysteries, not only confusing the enemy, but empowering us to pray effectively even when we don't know what to pray. It also edifies the one praying, strengthening his or her faith (Jude 1:20). This increased ability to pray, to confuse the enemy, and to strengthen our faith makes tongues powerful ammunition for our lives and ministry.

7. *Practice praise.* Hebrews 13:15 admonishes us to continually offer our sacrifice of praise—the fruit of our lips—to God. This admonition means more than just being thankful, for thanksgiving is actually both offensive and defensive warfare against the demonic army. The offensive nature of praise is exemplified in the story of Jehoshaphat (2 Chronicles 20). On the defensive side, praise is compared to one of the most significant defensive structures of biblical times: the gates of a city. God will be the defender; the gates of the city will experience no destruction and the sound of violence is not heard (Isaiah 60:18).

8. *Cultivate right relationships.* Right, loving relationships with our family in Christ create a strong foundation on which we can walk without stumbling (1 John 2:9–11). In addition, 1 John 1:7 indicates that the blood of Jesus cleanses us from our sin as we walk in harmony with one another. Matthew 18:18–20 records Jesus' outline on maintaining proper relationships and ties this issue to several of the weapons used in deliverance (specifically the principles of binding and loosing and of agreement).

9. *Develop a dynamic faith.* Just as a lack of faith can be the basis for failure (Mark 9:18–19) and worries (Matthew 6:25–30), the presence of faith can be the source of victory (Matthew 9:22; Mark 10:52). To develop a dynamic faith, we must be careful about where we focus our attention. Both Mark and Luke record Christ's admonition to be careful of what we hear because to those who hear, more will be given (Mark 4:24; Luke 8:18). The importance of guarding our ears is further underscored when we recognize that faith comes by hearing and hearing by the Word of God (Romans 10:17).

10. *Practice confessing God's Word.* Not only do we need to heed God's Word to develop a strong and dynamic faith, but we also need to know His Word to the extent that it becomes part of us and flows out from us. To speak God's Word is to speak truth (John 17:17), and truth will always defeat the enemy's plans. Jesus taught, "You shall know the truth and the truth shall make you free" (John 8:32). Psalm 119:11 says, "Your Word have I hidden in my heart, / That I might not sin against You." By practicing confessing God's Word, we are both hearing the Word, which builds faith, and hiding it in our hearts. Luke 6:45 reminds us that out of the abundance of the heart the mouth speaks.

11. *Learn to crucify the flesh and resist the devil.* Remember that our adversary, the devil, desires to drag those who have been set free back into the same bondage. The flesh is a battleground, and it must be put to death daily. God's Word exhorts us to crucify our old self and reckon ourselves dead to sin (Romans 6:6–11). Paul conveys the struggle between flesh and spirit when he wrote that the things he desired to do he did not do, and the very things he desired not to do he did (Romans 7:19). The battle is constant, but as we learn to crucify the flesh, we also learn to withstand the enemy's temptations and attacks. James reminds us that when we resist the devil, he will flee from us (James 4:7). Our adversary may walk around as a roaring lion seeking to devour us, but if we remain steadfast and vigilant, we can overcome him (1 Peter 5:8–9).

12. *Avoid people who are a bad influence.* God's Word firmly maintains that friendship with the world is enmity with God (James 4:4). Numerous Scriptures instruct us not to associate with people whose influence will corrupt us. For example, Proverbs 22:24 advises, "Don't hang out with angry people" (*The Message*). This doesn't mean we should avoid or

reject unbelievers; after all, Jesus ministered to heathens and tax collectors—the untouchables of His culture. However, when we are trying to overcome the enemy and maintain our own personal freedom, it is wise not to hang out with people who will influence us to walk in bondage again.

13. *Submit to the Lord and those in authority.* Submission is not synonymous with obedience, both of which must be maintained if we are to keep our freedom. Submission connotes *willing obedience.* For example, a child who is told to sit down may obey but still not submit. He or she may sit down on the outside but *remain standing* on the inside. To maintain freedom, we must sit down both on the outside and on the inside. We cannot resist the enemy if we are not fully submitted to God. We should also humble ourselves and submit to those in authority so God can exalt us in His time (1 Peter 5:5–6).

14. *Maintain a daily prayer life.* The Lord's Prayer demonstrates that we are to ask our Father to deliver us from the evil one (Matthew 6:13). This same passage also tells us how regular our prayer life needs to be: "Give us this day our daily bread" (Matthew 6:11). Prayer is our spiritual sustenance, or bread, and it is to be part of our daily life.

15. *Remember you are wearing an armor of defense.* Ephesians 6:13–17 outfits believers with an arsenal of defensive armor. The belt of truth, breastplate of righteousness, shoes of peace, shield of faith, and helmet of salvation are all elements of a Christian's armor to protect him or her from enemy attack. Wearing this armor entails more than merely confessing it as ours: It means living our lives in accordance with the characteristics of Christ. For example, it doesn't suffice to say we are putting on the belt of truth; we must actually live our lives based on God's truth for the armor to operate effectively.

16. *Don't forget your access to the offensive weapons.* Ephesians 6:17–18 identifies two of the offensive weapons in our arsenal: the sword of the Spirit (God's Word) and prayer. The principles of binding and loosing and of agreement are also offensive tools, as well as applying Jesus' blood to our circumstances and using Jesus' name with the authority He gave every believer. Praise is another effective offensive weapon to drive back and defeat the enemy (as used by Jehoshaphat in 2 Chronicles 20).

17. *Maintain a disciplined life.* Paul stated that he disciplined his body and brought it into subjection so he would not be disqualified (1 Corinthians 9:27). To maintain our freedom we, too, must live disciplined lives. We must recognize that living our lives for the Lord has clear rewards and offers present victory, but God's Word never promises that it is an easy road. On the contrary, we are warned that the gate is narrow, the way is difficult, and few find it (Matthew 7:14).

18. *Fast regularly to keep the cutting edge in your life.* Jesus taught that fasting was one part of the disciplined Christian life. He also taught that fasting should not be done for others to recognize and see but in secret, so the Father can reward us openly (Matthew 6:16–18). Fasting is a practice of self-denial to honor the Lord. By practicing fasting, we are acknowledging our commitment to keep the Father and His will as our center. By pursuing this type of close relationship with Him, we are effectively averting and defeating the enemy's snares and traps.

The points identified in this chapter are by no means a conclusive list of every action that should be taken to maintain a believer's freedom, but they are a biblically based foundation upon which to build. These foundational principles should be considered the minimum standard imparted to any individual who would receive deliverance ministry. To put teaching such principles in perspective, consider the Old Testament example of the watchman:

> "'But if the watchman sees the sword coming and does not blow the trumpet, and the people are not warned, and the sword comes and takes any person from among them, he is taken away in his iniquity; but his blood I will require at the watchman's hand.'"
>
> —Ezekiel 33:6

Those who minister in any area, but particularly in deliverance, should consider themselves watchmen set upon the wall. If the warning is given and the people ignore it, then their blood is upon themselves. Those who minister deliverance should warn (or teach) those about to be delivered just what is required to maintain their freedom. If ministers fail to do so, the Lord may hold them responsible for any resulting damage.

Limitations in Ministry

O ne of the greatest dangers for novice deliverance ministers is that they will exceed the authority granted them
by God's Word. Deliverance is an act of warfare, and warfare
is military action. God's Word clearly indicates that He considers us soldiers in virtually every area of our lives. Paul not
only compares a believer to a soldier, but he also quite specifically and directly calls the believer a soldier:

> You therefore must endure hardship as a good sol-
> dier of Jesus Christ. No one engaged in warfare
> entangles himself with the affairs of this life, that he
> may please him who enlisted him as a soldier.
> —2 Timothy 2:3–4

Recognizing that we are soldiers, we become aware of the
danger of entangling ourselves with worldly affairs. Instead
of allowing *civilian* matters to distract us, we must strive to
act properly and under the command of the One who enlist-
ed us—Jesus Christ. As good soldiers, we are expected not
only to fight the good fight of faith (1 Timothy 6:12) but to
follow the orders of our Commanding Officer.

Believers have almost forgotten that army protocol is governed by rules of engagement, and these rules are provided to ensure both soldiers' and civilians' safety. Spiritual military life has its own rules of engagement so our army can be effective without causing collateral damage. Rules of engagement are typically codified and provided to each soldier so that he or she may know in advance how to handle a given situation. Just as with the natural structure of the military, God has His own rules of engagement as Commander in Chief of His spiritual army, and we are expected to obey both His written and oral directives.

God's rules of engagement are our guidelines for spiritual warfare. They inform us when to refrain from battle and when to press in. They train us for guerrilla warfare and sabotage. The following points are some fundamental areas in which believers should exercise caution when ministering deliverance or engaging in spiritual warfare. If unsuccessful in deliverance ministry, these are some of the first issues to examine.

VIOLATION OF AN INDIVIDUAL'S WILL

God created humans to have a degree of free will. How far that free will extends may be debatable, but its existence is unquestionable. In the Garden of Eden, humanity chose to exercise that free will and believe a serpent's lies over God's truth. As a result, sin entered the world and humanity's relationship with God was broken. This broken relationship allows Satan's demonic forces to harass, intimidate, and oppress or possess humankind.

Whenever we attempt to unseat a demonic entity from its throne of influence over a person, place, or thing, a battle must be waged. As we discussed earlier, both Christians and non-Christians can consent to evil influences in their lives. As a result, one of the first hurdles to overcome in deliverance ministry is to ensure that the person being ministered to actually wants to be free. This may seem to be a rather juvenile concern until we recognize how the enemy employs his primary weapon—deception.

The serpent's tactics were lies from the beginning. In the Garden, he convinced Eve that God's motives were questionable and she had nothing to lose and everything to gain by eating from the Tree of the Knowledge of Good and Evil. Since the enemy operates within the framework of deception, it should not be surprising that some individuals may be deceived into believing there is nothing from which they need to be freed, that they are perfectly fine just the way they are.

Deliverance will not benefit an individual who does not want to be free. Demons have no authority in a believer's life except what the believer has given them. To seek individuals' freedom from influences that will immediately be allowed to return is of no benefit whatsoever. Deliverance should never be ministered in a context where the individual has not purposefully expressed a desire to be free from demonic influence (either generally or specifically). The significance of error in this arena becomes painfully obvious when we consider Jesus' warning in Luke 11:24–26:

> "When an unclean spirit goes out of a man, he goes
> through dry places, seeking rest; and finding none,
> he says, 'I will return to my house from which I
> came.' And when he comes, he finds it swept and
> put in order. Then he goes and takes with him seven
> other spirits more wicked than himself, and they
> enter and dwell there; and the last state of that man
> is worse than the first."

Evil spirits do not simply leave and never return when commanded to do so. Quite the contrary, when they are driven out, they actively seek to return . . . with comrades. For unbelievers, this will result in worse bondage than before. Jesus referred to deliverance (and healing) as the "children's bread" because of this reason. It is unlikely unbelievers will understand how to avert the demonic entity's return, particularly when they do not have Christ to lean on for continued freedom.

The analogy used in the previous Scripture indicates that when the unclean spirit seeks to return to its former home, it is able to because those quarters are unoccupied. By extension, it would appear that in order to avoid the demon's return (along with seven more wicked spirits), the house must be found occupied.

The first step in occupation is for the believer to turn over dominion of that area of his or her life to the Holy Spirit. The next step is to allow the Holy Spirit to fill his or her life with love, joy, peace, and all the other fruits of the Spirit. Obviously, these are acts requiring decisions of the will. So, unwanted or nonconsensual deliverance often creates more problems than it solves and ultimately does more harm than good. But how can unwanted or nonconsensual deliverance even occur? If those ministering deliverance choose to exercise their authority over demons without the person receiving ministry having a true desire to be free, then he or she will make no effort to fill that empty space with the fruit and presence of the Holy Spirit and may even overtly, or subtly, welcome the demonic presence back into his or her life. And as Scripture (particularly Luke 11:24–26) attests, the latter state of that person will be worse than the first.

Two factors are at work here. First, believers have

authority to command demons to leave but not to ensure that they do not return (that is the responsibility of the person receiving ministry). Second, demons clearly know and understand God's Word and its principles (remember, Satan twisted God's Word to deceive Eve in the Garden [Genesis 2] and to tempt Jesus in the wilderness [Matthew 4]), so they may willingly depart until an opportune time to return in greater numbers.

LACK OF PREPARATION

Jesus is our role model. He discipled others in the works He preformed and demonstrated His authority to heal and deliver. Finally, He imparted His authority to them and sent them out two by two with power to heal and deliver. With this preparation and instruction, the disciples went out and were successful.

> So they went out and preached that people should repent. And they cast out many demons, and anointed with oil many who were sick, and healed them.
>
> —MARK 6:12–13

The achievements seen here in Mark 6 are directly related to the disciples' preparation before ministry. One reason for failure in ministering deliverance is the lack of preparation before stepping out in action. The disciples exercised authority over demons and cast out many of them, but there came a time when they were unsuccessful in their deliverance ministry.

> Then one of the crowd answered and said, "Teacher, I brought You my son, who has a mute spirit. And wherever it seizes him, it throws him down; he foams at the mouth, gnashes his teeth, and becomes

rigid. So I spoke to Your disciples, that they should cast it out, but they could not." He answered him and said, "O faithless generation, how long shall I be with you? How long shall I bear with you? Bring him to Me." Then they brought him to Him. And when he saw Him, immediately the spirit convulsed him, and he fell on the ground and wallowed, foaming at the mouth. So He asked his father, "How long has this been happening to him?" And he said, "From child-hood. And often he has thrown him both into the fire and into the water to destroy him. But if You can do anything, have compassion on us and help us." Jesus said to him, "If you can believe, all things are possi-ble to him who believes." Immediately the father of the child cried out and said with tears, "Lord, I believe; help my unbelief!" When Jesus saw that the people came running together, He rebuked the unclean spirit, saying to it: "Deaf and dumb spirit, I command you, come out of him and enter him no more!" Then the spirit cried out, convulsed him greatly, and came out of him. And he became as one dead, so that many said, "He is dead." But Jesus took him by the hand and lifted him up, and he arose. And when He had come into the house, His disciples asked Him privately, "Why could we not cast it out?" So He said to them, "This kind can come out by nothing but prayer and fasting."

—MARK 9:17–29

It's clear from this passage that the disciples had had an opportunity to cast out this spirit but were unsuccessful. Jesus, on the other hand, speaks and it is accomplished. When the disciples question Jesus privately about why they had been unsuccessful, He basically tells them they were unprepared.

Jesus' statement, "This kind can come out by nothing but prayer and fasting," reveals much more than just information on how to exorcise a specific type of demonic spirit. Jesus is showing the disciples that they had become complacent. The disciples presumed Jesus' authority was sufficient, when in reality, their own preparation for warfare was also significant. The preparation they lacked involved receiving marching orders and carrying those orders out. First, they had not spent the time necessary in prayer to know from God how to handle this specific situation. Second, they had not exercised self-discipline (fasting) to prepare themselves to accomplish the work.

Doubtless the Lord is merciful and often honors our efforts even when our preparation has been lacking, but we must also recognize that He expects a maturing process. We must graduate from milk to meat at a certain stage. There is a price to be paid in deliverance ministry if we enter a situation without proper preparation. If we find ourselves in an unforeseen spiritual battle, God will certainly uphold us; however, when we know we will face spiritual warfare, it is important to be adequately prepared so we can achieve victory easily and swiftly, with minimal casualties and damage.

USING YOUR OWN KNOWLEDGE

Lack of preparation can lead to serious faults in deliverance ministry. One of the most serious is ministering out of our own knowledge rather than God's revelation (eating from the Tree of the Knowledge of Good and Evil rather than the Tree of Life). When we fail to prepare, we will often fail to listen to what God is saying and look for what He is doing. God is not apprehended just by our intellect; even the demons believe in God and tremble (James 2:19).

Deliverance ministry tools such as lists of demonic strongholds, checklists to identify a person's sinful activities, written or memorized prayers, etc. can be beneficial in deliverance ministry, but it is also important to let God orchestrate each unique situation. Formulas and methodologies based on human knowledge may be useful as reminders, but they can never substitute for God's direction, for all can potentially fail, but God will not. One of the most famous biblical examples of following a format without divine input occurs in Acts 19:13–16:

> Then some of the itinerant Jewish exorcists took it upon themselves to call the name of the Lord Jesus over those who had evil spirits, saying, "We exorcise you by the Jesus whom Paul preaches." Also there were seven sons of Sceva, a Jewish chief priest, who did so. And the evil spirit answered and said, "Jesus I know, and Paul I know; but who are you?" Then the man in whom the evil spirit was leaped on them, overpowered them, and prevailed against them, so that they fled out of that house naked and wounded.

The lesson here is that invoking the name of Jesus held sufficient authority to cast out demonic powers—but not without dialogue and relationship with Jesus. Notice that when the seven sons of Sceva acted on information rather than communication, the enemy (or the demonic spirit) prevailed. Acting on presumption without relationship and revelation can seriously injure us, but when we walk in the fullness of the power and authority God has granted us, nothing can harm us (Luke 10:19).

Divine revelation provides breakthroughs in challenging

deliverance situations. Once while ministering to a woman who had been a high priestess in satanism, Bill and his ministry team had reached a dead end. However, during an afternoon walk in the woods, the Lord spoke to one of Bill's team members and told him to pull a flower from a dogwood tree. The Lord then identified four remaining demonic entities and associated each of them to a petal on the blossom. Finally, using the crown (pistil and stamen) in the middle of the flower, He identified the fifth demon that remained, which was recognized as the strongman in this woman's life. This revelation was the breakthrough needed to exorcise those demonic spirits. Applying human knowledge without divine revelation in such a situation would have severely hampered the effort to set this woman free.

REVILING THE ENEMY

An easy mistake in deliverance ministry is to be drawn into arguments with demonic entities. Demons often speak through individuals. It is important to distinguish throughout the deliverance session between the voice of the one being ministered to and the voices of the demonic entities speaking through him or her. Arguments with demons often begin with a simple exchange:

> Minister: "I command you to go in the name of Jesus."
> Demon: "I won't leave."
> Minister: "You have to leave."
> Demon: "I do not."
> Minister: "Yes, you do."
> Demon: "I won't go."
> Minister: "You must go."

It is not unusual for uninitiated and inexperienced

deliverance ministers to begin with a similar dialogue and before they've realized it, to be arguing rather than ministering. Such a situation is designed by the enemy to misdirect the interaction, create distraction, and belie the truth of God's Word and believers' authority. The enemy has succeeded in drawing attention away from Jesus and the authority of His name and has veered the focus onto the demonic entity and its will. Satanic forces will seize every opportunity to lie, provoke, and intimidate to maintain their positions.

Once an argument has been initiated by a demon, the minister then risks having an interchange of a reviling nature. A reviling conversation occurs when the exchange shifts to verbal abuse, scolding, quarreling, or angry rebukes. The minister at that point has been lured into the enemy's trap. The key scriptural admonition against this pitfall is Jude 1:9:

> Yet Michael the archangel, in contending with the
> devil, when he disputed about the body of Moses,
> dared not bring against him a reviling accusation,
> but said, "The Lord rebuke you!"

Refusing to engage in disparaging and scornful conversation keeps the focus of deliverance ministry on the authority of the Lord Jesus Christ. If the enemy can provoke the minister to agitation, anger, and frustration, then he can successfully thwart deliverance.

EXERCISING CELESTIAL AUTHORITY

Human beings, in our fallen state, have forever sought to dominate and control whatever we can. Frequently, though, we have attempted to wield authority where we have no "legal" right to intervene. Deliverance ministry is no exception, and the results can be devastating. God's Word proclaimed that in the beginning, humankind was given dominion over the earth (Genesis 1:26). However, nowhere in God's Word are we given dominion in the Heavens or over other human beings. One of the strictest limitations in deliverance ministry, and in spiritual warfare in general, is the biblical limitation on the human realm of authority.

When we seek to exercise authority where God has not granted it to us, we move ourselves outside the protective covering of God's grace and make ourselves vulnerable to the enemy's counterattacks. It is vital to remember that the basis of our authority is God's Word. There is a price to be paid and needless casualties may ensue when we attempt to exercise authority we do not hold. God's Word delineates the boundaries of human authority.

The initial grant of human authority happened in the Garden of Eden when God gave Adam dominion over the earth and all its inhabitants. It was a limited grant of authority, or, in legal terminology, a limited power of attorney. Adam and Eve's fall relinquished human dominion over the earth to Satan, a loss that could only be reversed through divine redemption. The finished work of Christ on the cross returned legal authority over the earth to God, and Jesus' sacrifice resulted in His exaltation, placing all authority in His hands.

And Jesus came and spoke to them, saying, "All authority has been given to me in heaven and in earth."

—MATTHEW 28:18

This statement clearly indicates at least two realms of authority: one in Heaven and one on earth. As disciples of Jesus, our authority is to be exercised in an earthly, not heavenly, context.

> "Assuredly, I say to you, whatever you bind on earth
> will be bound in heaven, and whatever you loose on
> earth will be loosed in heaven. Again I say to you
> that if two of you agree on earth concerning any-
> thing that they ask, it will be done for them by My
> Father in heaven."
>
> —MATTHEW 18:18–19

The authority given to believers to trample serpents and scorpions (symbolic of demons and devils) is earthly authority. We have the legal right to tread them under our feet. This indicates believers' absolute, earthly authority over demonic activity and, therefore, authority to minister deliverance. We have this right because the demonic entity has stepped into our realm of authority. However, we would be exceeding our authority if we attempted to rebuke or command demonic forces that have not entered this earthly realm. More specifically, in deliverance, we always have authority to command demons oppressing individuals to depart; however, we do not have the authority to come against a ruling principality that is overseeing a demonic onslaught from its second Heaven position (the demonic realm). Daniel 10 is the basis for this understanding:

> Suddenly, a hand touched me, which made me tremble
> on my knees and on the palms of my hands. And he
> said to me, "O Daniel, man greatly beloved, under-
> stand the words that I speak to you, and stand
> upright, for I have now been sent to you." While he
> was speaking this word to me, I stood trembling. Then

he said to me, "Do not fear, Daniel, for from the first day that you set your heart to understand, and to humble yourself before your God, your words were heard; and I have come because of your words. But the prince of the kingdom of Persia withstood me twenty-one days; and behold, Michael, one of the chief princes, came to help me, for I had been left alone there with the kings of Persia. Now I have come to make you understand what will happen to your people in the latter days, for the vision refers to many days yet to come . . . Do you know why I have come to you? And now I must return to fight with the prince of Persia; and when I have gone forth, indeed the prince of Greece will come. But I will tell you what is noted in the Scripture of Truth. (No one upholds me against these, except Michael your prince.)"

—DANIEL 10:10–14, 20–21

Notice in this passage that Daniel's prayers had no effect upon the warfare taking place in the Heavens. In fact, the answer to Daniel's prayer was delayed by that warfare. This angelic being speaking to Daniel acknowledges that he has come because of Daniel's words, yet those same words had been unable to impact the twenty-one-day demonic opposition. Apparently, Daniel commanded authority in the earthly realm but lacked it in the realm of the second Heaven. When the angelic being leaves Daniel to return to the battle, he notes that "no one" is available to assist him except the angel Michael. No one else has the authority to do so. Despite Daniel's limited authority, this warfare did not stop the answer to his prayer, for God has authority even in the second Heaven and can delegate it to whom He will (in this case, the angel Michael and the angel who visited Daniel).

Since we presently exist within the confines of the earthly realm, our authority mirrors that of Daniel; just as Daniel's impact on the second Heaven was limited, so are we limited in our spiritual warfare. Because we exist within the confines of the earthly realm, any demonic power that would oppress us must enter that realm and so becomes an open target of believers' spiritual warfare.

For detailed information on the limitations of spiritual warfare, we recommend John Paul Jackson's *Needless Casualties of War*, published by Streams Publishing House.

What Do I Do Now?

A s this book draws to a close, perhaps you are wondering, "What do I do now? How do I apply this information to real-life situations?" Three categories of people have read this book:

1. Those who are intrigued by what they've read and will ponder it in their hearts until the opportune time.
2. Those who are called to deliverance ministry and are ready to jump in with both feet.
3. Those who never want to hear the word *deliverance* again.

The Holy Spirit will direct the steps of the first two groups and bring those in need across their path. For members of the final group, though the Holy Spirit may test their willingness to act on His behalf, He will never force them to violate their will. No one has to use what he or she has learned in these pages; however, God has directed you to this book for a reason, and if you choose not to apply what you've read here, you and those you could have helped will miss out.

These principles will mature those who pursue them.

New understanding will come with each opportunity to touch the life of an individual the Lord brings to you. The following story, while somewhat humorous after the fact, illustrates the point that God's Word has layers of meaning, from the overtly practical to the deeply spiritual.

In the early days of his deliverance ministry, Bill did everything he perceived a "good" Christian minister should. Each time he ministered, he would follow the same pattern: Dressed nicely in slacks, dress shirt, and tie, he would greet the person seeking help and then begin ministry by bowing his head, closing his eyes, and praying. One day, while he was ministering in this manner, the young woman for whom he was praying, acting under demonic influence, calmly reached forward (unbeknownst to Bill, whose eyes were closed) and grabbed him by the tie, wrenching downward. Bill eventually freed himself from her grasp, but he learned a valuable lesson clearly stated in Scripture:

> "*Watch* therefore, and pray always that you may be counted worthy to escape all these things that will come to pass, and to stand before the Son of Man."
> —LUKE 21:36 (EMPHASIS ADDED)

This passage has taken on new meaning to Bill ever since. When ministering deliverance, never close your eyes, but watch while you pray so that you may escape the enemy's plans. If you are uncomfortable praying with your eyes open, you may wish to forgo the necktie!

> For God has not given us a spirit of fear, but of power and of love and of a sound mind.
> —2 TIMOTHY 1:7

Now that you have a clearer understanding of who your enemy is and what he does, you should be able to walk much more consistently in the practical application of this passage. True, we face a powerful, cunning adversary, but you need not fear him because God has given you authority over his power. In fact, knowing who he is and what he does should give you more confidence to oppose him. Even if the enemy were to exert every ounce of his strength, your power is greater; the love of God resident in your heart carries more authority, and the soundness of your mind enables you to confront him boldly. As a Christian, if you can fully apprehend this spiritual truth, then you need not fear the demonic having any impact on your life.

> "Heal the sick, cleanse the lepers, raise the dead, cast out demons. Freely you have received, freely give."
> —MATTHEW 10:8

What you have freely received needs to be freely given. As a believer, you have every right, and the responsibility, to help others understand what it takes to achieve and maintain freedom. Jesus never freed someone from a demonic strongman before he or she was ready. An important part of the deliverance process is understanding how to close—and also being willing to close—the door that was opened by our own sin or the sin of another. So, remember to teach and lead people to confess, repent, and forgive before utilizing the authority, power, and weapons at our disposal. God is not in the business of violating the free will of any individual, so for our weapons to be effective, those we minister to must want to be free. The desire for freedom is directly proportional to the willingness to prepare through confession, repentance, and forgiveness.

Finally, the Holy Spirit is the power that does the ministry, not us. If you truly understand this, you won't be distracted by arguments over whether or not a person has to speak in tongues, etc. You will be able to recognize the Holy Spirit's power, and you will find it much easier to handle the situations the Lord allows to come before you.

Deliverance ministry does not begin or end with commanding demons to go. In fact, preparation for ministry is perhaps more important than the actual ministry itself. The time spent preparing our heart is when the Lord fills us with the power we need to minister. Recognize that our adversary wants to distract us with the flaws that surface in those in need.

> Finally, brethren, whatever things are true, whatever
> things are noble, whatever things are just, whatever
> things are pure, whatever things are lovely, whatever
> things are of good report, if there is any virtue and
> if there is anything praiseworthy—meditate on these
> things.
>
> —PHILIPPIANS 4:8

By focusing on the true and praiseworthy, we can keep the proper heart attitude even when the people and circumstances around us are in turmoil.

Preparation and ministry are essential, but follow-up is also imperative. If we've securely laid the foundation from the beginning of the process, follow-up should be relatively simple. Usually, when someone begins to walk in true freedom, accompanying it is an innate desire to remain free.

Ultimately, even when basic training is over, every soldier must still follow the rules of engagement to remain *covered* by the Lord's protection. We must recognize that while God has given us tremendous freedom to act, function, and minister in His Name, we must honor the boundaries He has established if we are to be effective and safe. The boundaries for ministry identified in this book should not be viewed as restrictions but as guidelines that help us remain covered by the Lord's protection.

> He who dwells in the secret place of the Most High
> Shall abide under the shadow of the Almighty.
> I will say of the LORD, "He is my refuge and my
>   fortress;
> My God, in Him I will trust."
> —PSALM 91:1–2

I (Michael) wrote this chapter while sitting along the Gulf Coast of Alabama, listening to the sounds of the surf coming in and watching the waves toss themselves against the beach. An osprey (a large fish-eating bird resembling an eagle) flew past my window, up and down the beach, fishing. In that moment, the Lord spoke to me about how different individuals approach deliverance ministry. Some are like the waves crashing against the shore, He said, while others are like the osprey floating on the winds and searching for the right moment to plunge after its prey.

While the waves consistently, relentlessly pounded the shore, the Lord directed my attention to the osprey as an example of how a deliverance minister operates in the Spirit. He pointed out how the osprey soared, using its keen eyesight to search for fish just below the water's surface. Sometimes, it would dive toward the ocean, only to pull up and away at the last moment, without piercing the water. But then, suddenly, with clear determination, it plunged and almost disappeared into the sea. Although struggling, it soon emerged from the water and, with determined effort, lifted once again into the air, carrying its catch home to its nest.

The Lord told me He wanted us to approach deliverance ministry in the same way this bird had carried out its appointed task. To properly function in this ministry, you must be willing to float upon the wind of the Spirit and use the piercing eyes of your heart to delve below the surface of the lives that come your way. There will be times when you see people and know they are ready to be pulled from the enemy's clutches, yet when you approach them, they dart away into the depths and slip too far beneath the surface to be reached. But as you continue following the Spirit and watching for the opportunities the Lord will supply, the time will come when that determined plunge will bring freedom to the one the Lord has shown you. While it will no doubt require some degree of struggle, and at times the weight of this responsibility may seem greater than you can bear, perseverance will bring results. You will have the opportunity to lead people out of the darkness and home to the enveloping love of God.

Notes

CHAPTER 2

1. John R. Kohlenberger III and James A. Swanson, eds., *The Strongest Strong's Exhaustive Concordance of the Bible* (Grand Rapids: Zondervan, 2001).

CHAPTER 3

1. *Biblesoft's New Exhaustive Strong's Numbers and Concordance with Expanded Greek-Hebrew Dictionary* (Biblesoft and International Bible Translators, Inc., 1994).

2. Jewish tradition held that a parent was responsible for a child's keeping of the law until he or she reached adulthood. For a boy, this happened at the age of thirteen, and the celebration of this rite of passage is called *bar mitzvah* ("son of the commandment"), acknowledging that the child has now become accountable to keep the commandments himself. Otherwise, if the parent were still responsible for the child's keeping of the law, one could conclude that the parent's faith would suffice to set the child free.

CHAPTER 6

1. American Heritage Dictionary of the English Language (Boston: Houghton Mifflin Company, 2000).

About the Authors

BILL FRENCH is the founder of Advocate Ministries and has been involved in ministry for more than thirty years, with much of that time devoted to counseling those who have been involved in the occult. Bill has been married to his wife, Joyce, for fifty-three years. He has four children (Barry, Renee, Michael, and Leslee), eight grandchildren, and two great-great grandchildren. While his work as a counselor has ended, at his current age of eighty, he continues to travel and speak on issues related to overcoming the demonic and (as Bill likes to say) on the "whole counsel of the Word of God."

MICHAEL FRENCH, B.A., M.P.A., J.D., is pastor of Cahaba Christian Fellowship and president of Advocate Ministries. Michael has been involved in the work of Advocate Ministries for more than twenty years and planted CCF when he left a successful law practice to enter full-time ministry in 1998. Michael and his wife, Elisa, also serve as directors of Advocate's missions and pastoral training efforts in Africa. The couple has four children (Joshua, Caleb, Jacob, and Noah). Michael has a bachelor's degree in Political Science and a master's degree in Public Administration from

Jacksonville State University. He also has a Juris Doctorate from the University of Alabama. Michael travels and teaches around the world on various topics and serves as a teacher/instructor with both Advocate Institute and Streams Ministries Institute for Spiritual Development.

NEEDLESS CASUALTIES OF WAR

Unlock the secrets of effective spiritual warfare. Discover
foundational truths that will help you fight with wisdom
and authority. John Paul Jackson offers a theology of
spiritual warfare that is so simple, yet so profound.
Foreword by John Sandford.

To order, call Streams Ministries International at
1.888.441.8080.